DIAMONDS

DIAMONDS

A CENTURY OF SPECTACULAR JEWELS

PENNY PRODDOW AND MARION FASEL

PHOTOGRAPHY BY DAVID BEHL

HARRY N. ABRAMS, INC., PUBLISHERS

Project Manager: Robert Morton

Editor: Lory Frankel

Designer: Carol Robson

Rights and Permissions: Neil Ryder Hoos, Catherine Ruello

On pages 2–3: Diamond and platinum dragonfly brooch with ruby eyes by Fred Leighton, 1990s

Library of Congress Cataloging-in-Publication Data

Proddow, Penny.
 Diamonds : a century of spectacular jewels / Penny Proddow and Marion Fasel ;
photographs by David Behl.
  p. cm.
 Includes bibliographical references and index.
 ISBN 0–8109–3229–6 (hardcover)
 1. Diamonds. I. Fasel, Marion. II. Title.
TS753.P76 1996
739.27—dc20   96–3548

Published in 1996 by Harry N. Abrams, Incorporated, New York
A Times Mirror Company
All rights reserved. No part of the contents of this book may be
reproduced without the written permission of the publisher
Printed and bound in Japan

CONTENTS

A 1926 advertisement for the New York jeweler Marcus & Company entitled "That Unconquerable Crystal" featured this original woodcut by the artist Rockwell Kent. The text began, "Century after century, the diamond continues to receive the admiration and affection of people in every corner of the earth. Its superb beauty is easily apparent. Its desirability is universally admitted. There is a steady and insistent demand for it. And it has won its place fairly, for the diamond retains unchangingly and permanently, through the years, its unmatched light and brilliance."

I N T R O D U C T I O N

Though no one knows exactly when diamonds were first used for adornment, the gem has been highly valued since time immemorial. Composed of pure carbon with a supremely strong crystal structure, it is harder than any other stone. The Greeks admired this quality and they named the diamond *adamas*, which means unconquerable. Pliny the Elder, a Roman essayist, wrote in *Natural History* during the first century A.D., "The diamond, known for a long time only to kings and then to very few of them, has greater value than any other human possession, and not merely than any other gemstone."

The Old Testament book of Exodus lists *adamas* among the stones set in the Urim and Thummim, the breastplate of the Hebrew high priest. This may be the first reference to someone wearing *adamas*, as some contend, or it may refer to another hard gem. In any case, there is tangible evidence that ancient Romans wore rings with diamonds in their natural octahedron form (resembling two pyramids attached at the base). By the sixteenth century, primitive diamond cuts such as the point cut (half an octahedron) and the table cut (a point cut without the point) had been developed, and small diamonds showed up more frequently in jewelry, but these rare stones never composed entire jewels. Parceled out a few at a time, they were set in gold and enamel accessories.

Jewelry with diamonds as the principal material appeared for the first time in the seventeenth century, when merchant-travelers like Jean-Baptiste Tavernier, who supplied Louis XIV with diamonds, journeyed between Paris and the Golconda mines in India. During this period diamond cuts advanced significantly. The two primary shapes were an improved table cut and the rose cut, a gem with a flat base and triangular facets tapering to a point on top like a rosebud. The small planar surfaces bounced light around within the gem and made it twinkle. The eighteenth-century brilliant cut introduced facets on the bottom of the gem, or pavilion, releasing even more light.

As only kings could afford to buy enough diamonds to create a style, royalty dictated diamond jewelry fashions. The French crown jewelers rose to preeminence, universally respected and imitated for their magnificent diamond jewelry style. Established at the time of Louis XIV, the Versailles code of motifs—bows, ribbons, swags, and flowers—was judged the only repertoire of designs fit for formal diamond jewelry, and this style remained virtually the same until the nineteenth century. Even then, it changed slowly, in subtle ways.

The auction of the Diamonds of the Crown of France in 1887 marked a turning point in the history of diamond jewelry—the beginning of the modern age. Sold by a republican government at public auction, these symbols of a vanished monarchy ended up largely in the hands of Tiffany & Co. The American firm's success in obtaining the lion's share of the French crown jewels signified a shift in the client base of precious jewelers. Up to this time, jewelers with a single court appointment had plenty of work to sustain them. After the sale, jewelers had to be more competitive to meet the pace of change and the demands from varied clients, who included potentates and wealthy entrepreneurs, stage and screen stars. In addition, jewelers had to stay on top of new technologies and materials, mastering them quickly in order to keep their output current.

Working in their favor was an abundant supply of diamonds. The Golconda mines and the Brazilian mines (discovered in 1726) had been exhausted since the end of the eighteenth century. The South African mines ended the drought and produced quantities of diamonds for the early years of the twentieth century. Since then, diamond resources in over twenty countries have continued to make the gem available. Canary and pink diamonds from Africa and Australia respectively have arrived in sufficient quantity to create a movement in colored diamond jewelry for the first time.

A bounty of the gem has made the twentieth century rich in diamond jewelry. Styles from 1887 to 1995, to which this book is devoted, show more range than any other period in history, from regal looks to minimal diamond fashions, from big-ticket blockbusters to artistic decorations. As Nicola Bulgari commented, "The diamond is the common denominator of jewelry." It would be difficult—if not impossible—to review a century's worth of work through the emerald, ruby, or sapphire. The pure white and sheer sparkle of the diamond have proved complimentary to every style, none of which has failed to make use of the gem. The diamond's long association with preciousness contributes to its staying power, but its beauty cinches its success.

The diamond has been mesmeric since its discovery as a rough octahedron. Countless texts have analyzed its gemological properties. Big "name" diamonds in royal collections and museums have been documented extensively. But the diamond in its most steady role as a material in jewelry has been overlooked. This book charts modern diamond jewelry styles and the best and most innovative jewelers who set them ablaze.

DIAMONDS

CHAPTER 1

DIAMONDS OF THE CROWN OF FRANCE ON THE AUCTION BLOCK

The Crown Jewels! Are these words not worth a hundred lines of verse? What a mass of pictures they bring to our minds; what memories they evoke in us! At the very sound of them we see pass before our eyes, as in some brilliant pageant, triumphant kings, victorious emperors, the majesty of queens, the youth and beauty of princesses, and the splendor of those gala nights, sparkling with riches amassed over centuries, the brilliance made brighter still by the addition of all the riches of France, concentrated, as it were, in the sovereign's court. Those times are no more."

Louis Enault, *The Diamonds of the Crown*
(Paris: Editions Bernard et Cie, 1884)

Empress Eugénie's flamboyant diamond bow, interwoven with an ivy pattern, is mounted in silver and backed by gold. Eugénie tampered with all her jewelry, and this piece was no exception. Kramer made the bow in 1855 as the buckle of a diamond belt. Later, the empress asked one of her jewelers to make the bow more extravagant. The addition of five diamond streamers with daggerlike terminals, called pampilles, and a pair of diamond ribbons ending in tassels lengthened the bow into an 8½ -inch-long jewel that Eugénie wore as a stomacher, a decoration pinned onto the décolletage that extended down to the waist. At the auction of the Diamonds of the Crown of France in 1887 the stomacher was bought by Schlessinger and then sold to a prominent American family.

In 1887 diamond jewelry that had once been the exclusive property of French kings and queens became available to the highest bidders at an auction in Paris. While emeralds, sapphires, pearls, and semiprecious stones also figured in the lots to be sold, it was the diamonds that gave the collection its name, the "Diamants de la Couronne de France"—the Diamonds of the Crown of France. Though diamond jewels belonging to nobility had certainly been sold publicly before, this sale was different. It offered some of the most coveted diamonds to be found anywhere. But more than just an occasion to acquire big stones, the sale presented an education in what the finest jewelry of France, if not the world, looked like. The designs had an impact on the jewelers of the era and they went on to influence jewelers throughout the twentieth century. Few would dispute that the pieces in the collection rank among the most important examples of diamond jewelry ever made.

A jeweler responsible for numerous pieces in the collection, Bapst attended the auction, anxious to buy back some of its greatest creations. But it faced an intimidating array of competitors. Successful and ambitious jewelers from far and wide had come to bid on this treasure trove. The rising star of the French jewelry industry, Frédéric Boucheron, made a notable presence in the audience. Bonynge, representing the English crown, was there. And Tiffany & Co. came from the United States, willing to spend a great deal of money to bring famous Old World diamonds and crown jewels to the New World.

Also bidding against the jewelers were several members of the French royal family and of the monarchist parties who opposed the Third Republic, which had organized the sale. The Third Republic had come into power in 1871 after the fall of Napoleon III with only a slight margin of victory. Republicans lived in constant fear of a monarchist restoration, whether by Bourbons, Orleanists, or Bonapartists. Anybody whose family had worn the jewels might suddenly claim them—and the political power they represented—if they remained in the French treasury.

Certainly, the history of the collection was inseparable from the monarchy, its splendor and its politics. Francois I had established the French crown jewels after being forced to hand over his own jewels as ransom dur-

Empress Eugénie Surrounded by Her Ladies-in-Waiting, an 1855 painting by Franz Xaver Winterhalter, captures the pleasure-loving spirit of the Second Empire and provides a view of the often copied and frequently referenced Second Empire fashions. Gathered in a bower, the noblewomen wear enormous dresses puffed up with crinolines and accessorized by daytime gold revivalist jewelry, neck velvets, and pearls. Holding a bouquet of violets and swathed in a white and purple gown, Eugénie is the focal point of the gathering.

ing an Italian campaign in 1525. He filled the collection with the jewels of his wife, Queen Claude. In an emergency, the decorations could be converted into currency through outright sales. They could also be used as collateral for loans. The rest of the time, when worn by the king, queen, and court, the jewels emblazoned the glory of France on the minds of their subjects and foreign dignitaries.

Subsequent kings added to the holdings. Louis XIV acquired many large diamonds that became celebrated. In addition to the famous blue diamond later renamed the Hope (the gem was stolen from the treasury in 1792), he contributed the Grand Mazarin, the Mirror of Portugal, the Sancy, and other gems. The courts of Louis XV and Louis XVI set quantities of diamonds in silver. The metal was chosen for its color, which intensified the light of the gems. A gold backing prevented the silver oxidation from rubbing off on the skin of the wearer. The diamonds and metals were worked into romantic jewelry for women featuring bows, tassels, flowers, and feathers—making up the Versailles code of jewelry motifs. These motifs, along with swirling, openwork patterns of vines, tendrils, and flowers, decorated shield-shaped brooches and corsage ornaments up to six inches long. Tripartite jewels were also popular. A typical earring or brooch would have a button top, central bow, ribbon, or feather, and a pear-shaped pendant. The girandole design, a hallmark of the eighteenth century, resulted in brooches and earrings that resembled upside-down chandeliers with three pear-shaped diamond pendants.

These magnificent designs earned the French a status superior to jewelers worldwide, who looked to the French for ideas. The Louis styles were also used as a reference by the last person to put her imprint on the French crown jewels, Empress Eugénie, wife of Napoleon III. Dismantling many of the diamond pieces in the crown collection, she gathered all the gems together and commissioned a white style from Parisian court jewelers. Eugénie's collection had an array of bows, stars, crescents, flowers, neoclassical motifs, and pampilles (streamers of tapering diamonds with daggerlike terminals)—a dazzling blend of what the empress admired in the historic jewels of her predecessors and the most fashionable contemporary looks. It was this link with fashion that gave the government its principal argument for the sale.

Purposely overlooking the aesthetics and history of the collection, the Third Republic built a case to get rid of the jewels by labeling them frivolous. A deputy proclaimed from the corridors of power, "A democracy that is sure of itself and confident in the future has a duty to rid itself of these objects of luxury, devoid of usefulness and moral worth" (Bernard Morel, *The French Crown Jewels*, Antwerp, 1988, p. 369). The government considered disposing of the jewels at a raffle with a range of ticket prices, but dropped this idea for logistical reasons. On January 11, 1887, a decision was reached: these symbols of the monarchy would be sold at a public auction.

As expected, the Orleanists, Legitimists, and Bonapartists raised their voices in protest. The loudest outcries, however, came from another quarter: French jewelers, speaking out for their art. Acting as a spokesman, the chairman of the Chambre Syndicale de la Bijouterie, de la Joaillerie et de

Berthaud, the photographer chosen by the French government to shoot the Diamonds of the Crown for the auction catalogue, is shown hard at work in this behind-the-scenes view. The men and women at the table are making an inventory of the jewelry for the sale. Unfortunately, their work for the catalogue was riddled with errors, such as the inaccurate labeling of several name diamonds. The image was published in *L'Illustration* on February 19, 1887, as part of the hype surrounding the sale.

l'Orfèvrerie pleaded eloquently with the minister of finance: "Sir, the jewels known as the Crown Jewels are considered by our Master Jewellers, leaving aside the question of the value of the gems they bear, to be remarkable examples of workmanship, taste and perfection of execution—in a word, to be records of great value to the jewellery industry" (Morel, p. 370).

The government agreed to set aside a small group of jewels and important gems to be held in perpetuity by the state. The 140.64-carat Regent diamond was an obvious choice. It had been purchased by Louis XV and revered by all leaders. Napoleon had underwritten the cost of his army by pledging the Regent to an Amsterdam banker. After his victory he considered the diamond a good-luck charm and wore it in the hilt of his sword. Charles X's diamond-encrusted coronation sword was another historical

The Diamonds of the Crown of France were shown to the public for the first time at the 1878 Paris Exposition Universelle. The leaders of the Third Republic had mixed emotions about the crown jewels and their power to elicit sympathy for the monarchy. Nevertheless, they could not resist the opportunity to flaunt the superiority of France in the jewelry arts. For security reasons, the interior of the case was lowered into a basement vault after visiting hours.

item. From Empress Eugénie's diamond jewelry collection the government preserved one brooch set with two Mazarins, diamonds from the reign of Louis XIV. Everything the government kept was housed in the Muséum d'Histoire Naturelle, the Higher National School of Mines, or the Louvre.

While pacifying the jewelers with this gesture, the government made another decision that dismayed them even more: it broke apart many jewels, selling various segments as well as loose gems. The comb à pampilles made by Bapst in 1856 for Eugénie to wear on the occasion of the imperial prince's christening was broken into eighteen separate lots. Some lots included groups of diamonds, while others consisted of individual name stones. Probably the best single stones from the comb à pampilles were the light pink Hortensia diamond of 21.32 carats, the 17.4-carat King of Sardinia diamond, and a 13.61-carat marquise-cut diamond bought by Louis XIV from the traveler and diamond dealer Jean-Baptiste Tavernier.

When they saw their cause was lost, the jewelers lobbied for photographs, drawings, casts—anything that would preserve these treasures of France's ascendancy in the jeweled arts. Acceding to their demands for visual records, the government commissioned the photographer Berthaud to take photographs. Ironically, this proved disastrous to the industry that had made it happen. The documentary images, some taken before the jewels were broken up and some taken afterward, were then grouped together in a catalogue, which was sent out to prospective bidders—diamond dealers, importers, and jewelers around the world. The pictures were also given to magazines. The French publication *L'Illustration* (February 19, 1887) even featured behind-the-scenes shots of Berthaud's photography session at the Ministry of Finance.

This blitz of promotion was far from what the French jewelers had in mind. They wanted the records to remain on French soil for posterity, preferably locked up as tightly as the jewels, had they been kept. Instead, the Republic handed the French jewelers' competitors a precise sourcebook of designs to copy. Jewelers had been imitating French jewelry since the eighteenth century. With Berthaud's set of photographs at their side, giving them close-up views of these beautifully executed jewels by the greatest French jewelers, including, of course, Bapst, as well as Mellerio, Nitot, Gabriel Lemonnier, and Kramer, they were imbued with fresh enthusiasm.

As soon as the catalogues were distributed, jewelers started manufacturing the pieces practically diamond for diamond. The American trade organ the *Jewelers' Circular* reported that Alfred H. Smith & Co., a New York diamond importer, had a copy of the catalogue and "cordially invite[d] their friends and patrons to call and examine them," an open invitation to commission their own versions of Eugénie's jewels. The bowknots by Bapst were knocked off in quantity. Around 1900 Cartier acquired the original ones and created a line of Cartier bowknots. Even though Eugénie was not the first to wear stars, crescents, and flower heads, her collection certainly contributed to their longevity. Paradoxically, the Third Republic's destruction of some jewels affected jewelers' copies. Brooches that looked suspiciously like segments of Eugénie's diamond girdles began to appear in fashionable society.

Even before they gathered in the state rooms of the Louvre on May 12, 1887, the French jewelers saw what they regarded as rightfully theirs—the coveted Versailles court style—disseminated to the four corners of the world. Meanwhile, for the nine sessions of the auction, to May 23, jewelers came from all over Europe—Spain, Italy, Belgium, Holland, Portugal, Switzerland, and some from Denmark, Sweden, and Norway. The Russian appetite for diamonds being second only to that of the French court, the czar's jewelers made their way to France expressly for the sale, as did others from outposts on the trade routes of the Bosphorus, Nile, and the deserts of North Africa. For those nine days of the auction, gem dealers from Turkey, Egypt, and Tunis mingled with their European colleagues. The swelling crowd was rounded out with jewelers to the sugar barons of Havana. They all came to take advantage of the large number of fine and important gems. Although diamonds had been discovered in South Africa in the 1870s, mak-

For the auction, Empress Eugénie's corsage decoration of two bowknots suspending four strands of diamonds was broken down into one multistrand necklace and a pair of brooches. The necklace was the highest priced item in the sale, bought by Tiffany for Mrs. Joseph Pulitzer. The bowknots proved to be the most popular jewels in the collection. After they were published and put on public display, imitations appeared ad infinitum.

An anonymous jeweler made this fine copy of Empress Eugénie's bowknots shortly after the auction.

ing small stones readily available to international dealers, medium- and large-size diamonds were still rare. The auction offered an unusually high number of such diamonds. Oversize gems studded Eugénie's jewels. Good-size diamonds also characterized the royal orders and insignias, such as the Order of the Golden Fleece and the Legion of Honor. Although unwilling to donate the awards of merit to even one of the three museums, the Third Republic had to acknowledge the impropriety of selling them off intact to the highest bidder. So they broke them down into lots of loose diamonds.

Confirming the fears of the Third Republic, the Orleanists, members of the French royal family, arrived to bid on what they considered their legacy. But, competing with a formidable cross section of jewelers eager to purchase the exceptional goods, they were unable to retrieve enough to outfit a king or a queen. Some of these jewelers had links with royalty; others had their sights fixed on nonroyal clients and needed merchandise.

Nothing could have kept the French crown jeweler Bapst from the bidding floor. In a city famous for jewelers, Bapst was *the* jeweler to Empress Eugénie, with a long history of serving the crown of France. A member of the Bapst clan had purveyed jewels to the crown since 1734, during the reign of Louis XV. The Bapsts had been confidants to the royal family. Above and beyond the responsibility of creating magnificent formal wear, on different occasions they were entrusted with the honor and responsibility of taking the inventory of the treasury and arranging security precautions for the valuables. During the Franco-Prussian War, Bapst helped save the French crown jewels from certain destruction by assisting in their removal to the Bank of France in Brest.

Having failed to preserve its magnificent handiwork for posterity by stopping the auction, Bapst took to the floor and became an intimidating contender in bidding for possession of the jewels it had created. On the top of its list was the diamond Greek diadem. The firm had made three versions over the years, from 1856 to 1867, before the design met with the empress's final approval. The firm rushed this third one through production in fifteen days to have it ready for an evening at the opera. Eugénie was so thrilled with Bapst's magnificent concoction that she invited Paul Bapst and every artisan who had worked on it to the gala so they could see her wear it. The artisans took their seats in the balcony early, but Bapst, arriving late, was barred at the gates by the police: an assassination attempt had been made on the sovereigns, and some of the guards were wounded while protecting the couple. When the emperor and empress finally entered the imperial box, the audience gave them an overwhelming ovation. At this moment Eugénie stood. In gratitude for the applause and the heroism of those who had been injured saving her life, she lifted the collar of her cape and instinctively kissed the blood that had spattered it in the confrontation. The artisans of Bapst saw the grandeur of their handiwork and never forgot the momentous occasion. In homage to the crown of France, Bapst paid 135,500 francs for the tiara at auction.

Bapst's adversaries in the aisle also had ties to royal families. Representing the English crown, the jeweler Bonynge bought the aiguillettes and foundation ornament by Bapst for 21,100 francs. Seventy-seven diamonds composed the pampilles and sixty-seven diamonds in a range of sizes made up its bell-shaped crown, representing over 160 carats in all. The regal decoration went into the hands of the English nobility as a treasured keepsake of the French royal family.

An up-and-coming jeweler, Frédéric Boucheron came to the auction hoping to buy the Grand Mazarin, one of the finest name diamonds in the collection. His firm, established only twenty-four years earlier, already was a significant rival to older firms by virtue of its superior craftsmanship and innovative technology. C. Bordinckx, Boucheron's lapidary, had made a specialty of carving diamonds, a terrific feat.

A page from Bapst's workshop logbook shows the inventory of gems and an annotated design for the second version of Empress Eugénie's diamond Greek tiara made in 1864. Bapst bought back the third version of this jewel at the auction.

Representing the British royal family, the jeweler Bonynge paid 25,100 francs at the auction for one of Eugénie's jewels made by Bapst in 1868 and referred to in the catalogue as the "aiguillettes and foundation ornament." Eugénie's aiguillettes and foundation ornament is a pendant with a bell-shaped crown of diamonds suspending diamond aiguillettes (pampilles clustered in a group). When it was worn, the jewel was attached to fabric or connected to another jewel by a loop behind the top stud.

When Boucheron won the Grand Mazarin at the sale, he was elated. The approximately 18.5-carat diamond was one of eighteen diamonds, ranging in size from 8 to 54 carats, that had been bequeathed to Louis XIV by Cardinal Mazarin in 1661. These diamonds formed the bedrock of the French crown diamond collection and could be traced through the various reigns of kings and emperors as the center stones of their most impressive jewels.

Even though Bapst, Boucheron, and others at the auction purchased some prized goods, they were probably unable to acquire as many as they had set their sights on. The American firm Tiffany & Co. was driving up the prices. The dark horse of the auction, Tiffany ultimately carried off more than a third of the merchandise. It bought loose stones, name diamonds, and

A ruby and carved diamond butterfly brooch by Boucheron is a masterpiece of French jewelry from the 1890s. Only a diamond can cut a diamond, but with the knowledge that it could be done, C. Bordinckx, Boucheron's lapidary, executed a unique line of diamond jewelry for the firm, creating signet rings with initials, crowns, and coats of arms. Carving on the table of a diamond, Bordinckx recreated a portrait of a woman after an original by Leonardo da Vinci. Jewels like these carved diamond pieces gave Boucheron its reputation for creativity.

jewelry, purchasing hundreds of years of history in an instant. The 29.22-carat De Guise went to the eager American bidder for 155,000 francs. The flat table-cut diamond had been acquired by Louis XIV in default of a loan. His wife, Queen Marie-Thérèse, wore it in a necklace of forty-five diamonds before Louis XV had it recut. Tiffany also bought the Fleur-de-Pêcher, a 25.53-carat pear-shaped diamond of pale pink color, for 128,000 francs. Originally purchased by Louis XIV in 1691, it had served as a center stone in a diamond tiara worn by Empress Marie-Louise, consort of Napoleon I.

Tiffany's apparent coup at the time was capturing four Mazarin diamonds. It has taken over a hundred years for the facts about these stones to be straightened out. Jewelry historian Bernard Morel revealed in *The French Crown Jewels* that these four gems had been inaccurately catalogued as Mazarins by the valuer at the time of the auction; because of their size and fine quality, the officials had assumed that they must be Mazarins. But if Tiffany did not get the authenticity it paid for with these diamonds, it did not necessarily matter. The firm probably would have bought them anyway. It was on a buying spree for big diamonds, name or no name. Another diamond, catalogued as the Mirror of Portugal, was returned to the auctioneers by a disgruntled buyer, Madame Gal, after Bapst told her it was not one of the

A drawing of the Girdle of Marie Antoinette notes the carat weights of the diamonds. The queen was accused of buying the diamond monstrosity from the jeweler Boëhmer et Bassenge with state money immediately before the Revolution of 1789. In fact, she turned the piece down, saying France needed a ship more than another jewel, but the revolutionaries refused to believe it. They considered her a spendthrift, and the episode only reinforced her reputation for frivolity, a word that would later be applied to Eugénie and cause the dispersal of the great diamonds of the crown. Although the concoction was never worn by the queen, the design was well-known to jewelers from this engraving, and some of the motifs can be found in turn-of-the-century jewelry. The pear-shaped diamond with a circular-cut diamond surround was a standard element in early-twentieth-century Cartier diamond and platinum pieces. Reportedly, the infamous jewel surfaced again during the 1848 political unrest in France, when Tiffany purchased it.

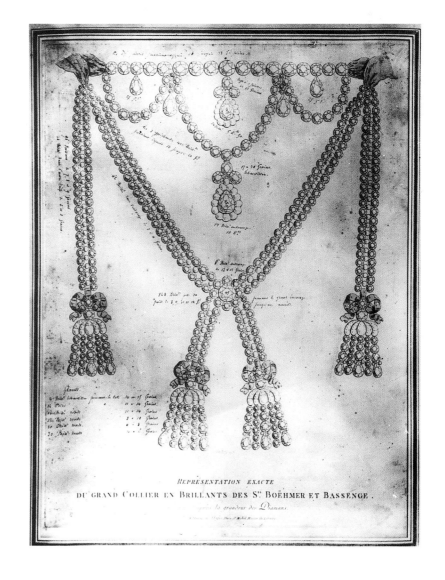

REPRESENTATION EXACTE
DU GRAND COLLIER EN BRILLANTS DES S.ᵗˢ BOËHMER ET BASSENGE.

Empress Eugénie's currant-leaf bodice decoration includes a 20.03-carat diamond. At the auction of the Diamonds of the Crown of France, Tiffany bought the extravaganza and sold it to Cornelia Bradley Martin.

For her 1897 Versailles Ball, Cornelia Bradley Martin accessorized a Mary, Queen of Scots, costume with three jewels from the auction of the Diamonds of the Crown of France. The most impressive is the all-diamond currant-leaf bodice decoration. The other two are the centerpiece from the great girdle (on her skirt) and two ruby and diamond bracelets (worn as a dog collar). A crisscross diamond stomacher accented with large pear-shaped diamonds, a belt of oversize diamonds, three long ropes of diamonds, a ruby and diamond quatrefoil brooch, a diamond sunburst brooch, and a diamond tiara complete the jewelry ensemble. New York hostess and member of the swanky Four Hundred, Bradley Martin hoped to lift spirits and help the city's economy during the 1896–97 financial crisis by giving a costume party at the Waldorf-Astoria and turning its Grand Ballroom into Versailles's Hall of Mirrors. The party and its theme—not to mention her husband, who dressed as Louis XV— succeeded in energizing the luxury trades, but its extravagance outraged the press. The Bradley Martins subsequently left New York to live in England.

Mazarins. Tiffany happily purchased the stone, because it was quite simply a fine diamond.

Tiffany also acquired several segments from the fabled Second Empire diamond girdles to sell as expensive souvenirs. These fabulous decorations, which covered the entire bodice, dipping over the full skirt and wrapping around the front and back, had been broken into segments to create manageable lots. Tiffany sold its segments in leather boxes embossed "Diamants de la Couronne" in gold on the top and "Tiffany & Co. New York and Paris" on the satin of the inner lid. In essence, it packaged a piece of history.

The firm founded in 1837 by Charles Lewis Tiffany that made a name for itself in silverware had acquired a taste for diamonds and diamond jewelry from Europe, the likes of which had never been sold in America before. In 1848 Tiffany's first partner, John Young, had a wildly successful buying trip when a visit to Paris coincided with a revolution and the rushed departure of King Louis Philippe and Queen Marie-Amélie. Young managed to buy sacks of diamond jewelry from retreating nobility desperate for cash. Among the loot was a piece purported to be the Girdle of Marie-Antoinette, a notorious jewel in French history.

In 1874 the manager of Tiffany's recently established branch in Paris, Gideon F. T. Reed, a Boston jeweler with a specialty in diamonds, acquired the most important lot at the auction of the estate of the Duke of Brunswick, an eccentric

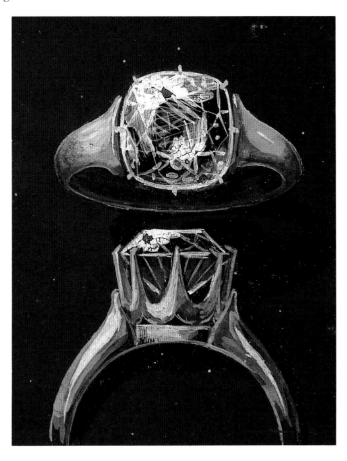

aristocrat who had a passion for antiquities and gems. The 30-carat canary diamond, which those in the know had been trying to wrest from the duke for years, was mounted in the eye of a platinum and gold peacock feather aigrette, the centerpiece of the Tiffany display at the Philadelphia Centennial Exhibition in 1876.

One hundred years after the American Revolution, fine diamonds, the pride of Europe, became the envy of Americans who had none to admire or study. No quality gem collections, like those of the British Museum in London, the Austrian Imperial Mineral Cabinet in Vienna, the Jardin des Plantes and the School of Mines in Paris, existed in the democratic United States. Tiffany had brought home the first name diamond ever to be seen in America by the public. Enthralled by the beauty of the gem, people flocked in record numbers to see it.

Eleven years later, at the auction of the Diamonds of the Crown of France, Tiffany had American heiresses waiting in the wings for jewels with star quality still intact. The currant-leaf corsage ornament by Bapst with a 20.03-carat diamond accent, which cost 120,100 francs, went to Cornelia Bradley Martin of New York. She also acquired two of Eugénie's ruby and

The original rendering for the Tiffany Setting was executed under Charles Lewis Tiffany's guidance in 1886. The setting was revolutionary at the time, because diamond rings had previously been mounted in bezel settings that encircled the diamond and concealed the pavilion, or bottom half of the gem. The prongs of the Tiffany Setting lifted the diamond up and allowed light to pass through the gem, heightening its brilliance. This invention took place around the time of the discovery of the South African diamond mines and the diamond euphoria generated by the sale of the French crown jewels. The setting was a key factor in establishing Tiffany as the greatest purveyor of diamonds in the United States.

diamond bracelets and the centerpiece from a girdle broken up for the auction. With what would be known ever after as "lot 10," a four-strand necklace of 222 diamonds by Bapst, Tiffany set the record price of the auction—183,000 francs. All of Paris found out who the new owner was when the wife of the publisher of the *New York World*, Mrs. Joseph Pulitzer, wore it to a ball in Paris immediately following the sale.

Individually, the Diamonds of the Crown of France were beautiful. Even in fragments they maintained their pomp. Taken as a collection, they enshrined the place of diamonds in formal jewelry, contributing to a high style that would be cyclically revived throughout the twentieth century. For design, the auction and its surrounding publicity made a collection of court jewels available for all to analyze and study. This was a first. Though jewelers may previously have been aware of a piece here and there, never before had they seen so large an array of royal property. Empress Eugénie's personal taste, with its connections to the great styles of the past—especially the courts of Louis XIV and Louis XV—became a guide for diamond jewelry throughout the twentieth century.

CHAPTER 2

ART NOUVEAU AND BIJOUX: DIAMONDS IN A SUPPORTING ROLE

Diamonds played a starring role in Empress Eugénie's jewelry sold at the auction of the Diamonds of the Crown of France, and after the dispersal of the collection, precious jewelers continued making accessories in a similar mode. Throughout the 1890s, they set diamonds in regal-looking Louis XV– and Louis XVI–style pieces designed to emphasize the gem's splendor. René Lalique was the jeweler who introduced a completely different style with nature and fantasy themes in which the means were subordinate to the artistic end. The style, later named Art Nouveau, included many different materials, especially enamel, that contributed to the jewel as a work of art. Lalique integrated diamonds into his enamel jewelry so completely that they shed all their previous associations with status and assumed a new character. In his hands they became artistic materials. That a jeweler like Lalique, working at the highest level of manufacturing, should use diamonds for their aesthetic rather than their intrinsic value constituted a dramatic change.

At the same time, diamonds propelled bijoux into a realm of higher intrinsic value and brought them to the attention of a precious jewelry clientele. A French word with no precise English equivalent, *bijoux* connoted at the turn of the century jewelry with an emphasis on design and craftsmanship. The figurative character of bijoux enabled its creators to engage in a certain give-and-take with the contemporary and historical fine arts and attracted sculptors and painters who wanted to extend their range to include jewelry. All of them wove popular themes into their work. Nature and religion were uppermost, followed by revivalist classical, Gothic, and Islamic imagery. Precious jewelers purchased work from the reservoirs of available talent or hired their own in-house specialists. The various partnerships of master craftsman or artist and precious jeweler led to imaginative small accessories that frequently carried dual signatures. This turn-of-the-century phenomenon was symbolic of the importance of the individual artistic talents to bijoux. The artisans who made bijoux specialized in different techniques: enamelwork, miniatures, carving in hard stone, and gold work. While most of the jewels centered on materials that were less than precious, the plentiful supply of diamonds from the first wave

In a pendant by Gabriel Falguières, a hard-stone carving of Orpheus's severed head, singing as it floats down a river to the sea, is encircled by a cresting wave of gold and diamonds. The jeweler's generous use of diamonds heightened the drama of the imagery.

of the South African rush made the gem available, and bijoux jewelers took advantage of the opportunity to use diamonds.

Lalique began his career selling jewelry designs in the prevalent modes to precious jewelers Aucoc, Cartier, Haemlin, Spaulding, and Tiffany and designed innovative diamond jewels for Boucheron and Vever before he revealed his original jewelry ideas under his own name at the 1892 exhibition "Les Arts de la Femme." Years later the *Jewelers' Circular* (February 3, 1904) reflected on the impact of the occasion: "he at once leaped into fame, and the style which he founded, began its rapid revolutionization of the French jewelry industry. His influence has been remarkable; he broke down the old barriers and demonstrated the importance of working on the broadest possible lines."

Some French jewelers paid Lalique the highest form of flattery by imitating his style and producing similar diamond and enamel work. In tribute to its source of inspiration, this jewelry was originally called Genre Lalique. But in a period of ferment, when winds of change were sweeping through design, Genre Lalique was quickly absorbed into a broader context. A dis-

In 1889 Lalique designed the singing bird brooch for Vever. Almost fully three-dimensional, the animated diamond birds with ruby eyes perch on a rose branch with leaves, flowers, and a butterfly. The piece is set in silver and gold. Before Lalique pioneered Art Nouveau jewelry, he designed imaginative gem-set jewelry like the singing birds for Vever as well as pieces for Boucheron, Cartier, and Tiffany. These jewels foreshadowed the sculptural direction his later work would take. The experience also gave him a familiarity with diamonds.

enchantment with period styles led decorative artists to pursue new designs for types of silver, furniture, ceramics, and textiles. Like Lalique, they were influenced by Japanese prints, and their work manifested a love of nature as well as sinuous lines with origins in landscape and a sweeping broken line called the whiplash. Many of these mavericks, including Lalique and jewelers like him, exhibited at Samuel Bing's Paris gallery L'Art Nouveau, which gave the name Art Nouveau to this turn-of-the-century movement in the decorative arts.

Lalique chose enamel as his primary material. This painterly substance, capable of graduated hues, linked his jewelry to the Impressionist painters, an aspect not lost on the critics. *Art et Décoration* (January–June, 1911, vol. 29, p. 27) pointed out that his pendants "can be called wonderfully delicious tableaus and certain tints of enamel are able to catch the reflection of light similar to passages in the paintings of Claude Monet and Sisley."

Diamonds served as counterpoints to enamel in Lalique's jewels. Technically speaking, he valued the way they refracted light. He enjoyed creating a variety of visual effects by experimenting with their placement. Small

Three dog collar plaques illustrate Lalique's dexterity with diamonds and enamel. Above, a gold sylph spreads her plique-à-jour enamel and diamond wings to fill the dog collar plaque. The gold veins of the wings and the crustaceous tail are lightly colored with a thin layer of transparent green enamel. The ethereal being seems made out of air and light, characteristic of her sphere. The dog collar plaque at center shows two revelers playing their pipes in a diamond woods. The design reveals the Japanese influence on Lalique's jewelry; it has no perspective point, the composition is flat, and the subjects are cropped on all sides. In the dog collar plaque below, the buds of a thistle make a pattern of color and texture in enamel. Far from a traditional feminine flower, its spiky stem inspired Lalique, who emphasized its prickles by delineating them in diamonds.

A long diamond stem
gives a vertical axis
to a stylized gold flower
pendant by Vever and
guides the eye from the
plique-à-jour enamel
leaves to the dangling
opal flower heads.

clusters of diamonds highlighted the wings of wasps, peacocks, and soaring fantasy creatures. Flat expanses of diamonds were set densely in landscape scenes defining water, earth, and vegetation. And single diamonds formed the stigmas and buds of flowers as well as the bodies of nuts bursting from their hard caps.

Lalique's natural world was a passionate place with elements of wildness and serenity. No garden-variety flowers lived here; such plantings as thistles with bristling stingers, Japanese cherry trees with clouds of blossoms, exotic orchids, and sycamore seedpods populated the jeweler's paradise. Lalique's jewels depicting the human figure swung between the extremes of ecstasy and chastity. Classical nymphs, bacchantes, and sylphs expressed uninhibited joy while medieval saints, angels, and nuns exuded a contemplative quiet and purity.

Lalique's designs broke the passivity of jewelry. By emphasizing drama, he put an emotional spin on jewelry that outraged some and delighted others. His subject matter went way beyond the typical whiplash line of the movement, favored by the decorative artists. Lalique contributed entirely different themes to Art Nouveau—the "new art."

Art Nouveau jewelry quickly won the approval of the official French jewelry association, the Chambre Syndicale de la Bijouterie, de la Joaillerie et de l'Orfèvrerie. Its support stemmed in part from a desire to distance itself from the Louis XV and Louis XVI diamond styles, which recalled the all-too-recent fiasco of the sale of the Diamonds of the Crown. In addition, it wanted to encourage the trade to create new jewelry for a new century.

Beyond France, Lalique and the Art Nouveau jewelers proved that artistic jewelry with enamel and diamonds could compete with all-diamond jewelry on the international exhibition circuit. In Turin, Saint Petersburg, London, and Saint Louis, critics were exuberant in their praise. The regularity of the exhibitions kept Art Nouveau uppermost in the trade publications and decorative arts magazines, such as *Art et Décoration*. This prestigious periodical began covering jewelry for the first time around 1895, when Art Nouveau jewelry was shown alongside the decorative arts at the Salons of La Société des Artistes Français.

In reviews and texts, Lalique was always singled out for his superior achievements, often to the detriment of his colleagues. Henri Vever wrote in his 1898 diary, "Lalique is always splendid and the others very mediocre." Indeed, others had difficulty competing when they were accused of stealing Lalique's shapes, subjects, and materials. However, several master jewelers carved out reputations for outstanding work. René Foy and Gaston Lafitte consistently won recognition at exhibitions for their contribution to the movement. Gabriel Falguières, a skilled craftsman who produced diamond jewelry for a number of the best Parisian firms during the Second Empire and Third Republic, did not relinquish diamonds for his narrative Art Nouveau pieces but used them to good effect as dramatic decoration. Alphonse Auger adroitly meshed his goldsmithing background with Art Nouveau plique-à-jour enamel. Georges Fouquet fully embraced the new style by hiring Alphonse Mucha, Sarah Bernhardt's artistic director, to redesign his salon and contribute jewelry designs to his display at the 1900 Paris Exposition Universelle.

One of the few considered to be Lalique's equal, Lucien Gaillard imported Japanese craftsmen to replicate the favored look. Henri and Ernest Vever created some superior examples of the style, using diamonds as a rhythmic trail through the multiple planes of their sometimes delicate, more often highly sculptural, enamel jewelry. At what is considered the most important Art Nouveau milestone, the 1900 Paris exposition, Vever shared the grand prix with Lalique.

Though Art Nouveau was an enormous critical success, it was not a commercial success. The jewelers found it too labor-intensive to generate enough profit, while the clients discovered that many of the pieces were too fragile to wear. After the 1900 exposition, Art Nouveau jewelry was knocked off and mass-produced by lesser jewelers. Imitations lacking fine craftsmanship flooded the market and contributed to its rapid demise; the movement was dead by World War I. However, no history of diamond jewelry would be complete without mentioning Art Nouveau. It had an undeniable impact on artistry in all jewelry. And the diamond Louis XV and Louis XVI styles purveyed by jewelers around the world changed as a result of it. The *Jewelers' Circular* (February 3, 1904) succinctly summed up the consequences of Art Nouveau: "The productions of the future in which the diamond or other expensive gems play a part, will be of a lighter and more artistic nature."

Unlike the Art Nouveau jewelers, bijoux jewelers had no interest in abandoning the past. In fact, many of them worked with old techniques—miniatures and scrimshaw—and brought old forms, like cameos and portrait medals, to jewelry. Their designs were straightforward in comparison with

A diamond and platinum brooch encases butterfly wings in crystal. Bijoux jewelers mixed unorthodox materials with diamonds. The anonymous Frenchman who made this piece went so far as to incorporate actual butterfly wings in the design.

the expressive work of the Art Nouveau jewelers. With the exception of Tiffany's 1889 collection of orchids, bijoux did not compete with formal diamond styles. These pretty little diamond-studded tokens filled out a jeweler's inventory, providing small items for gift giving.

Almost an exact replication, the 1889s spread petal orchid brooch by Tiffany, measuring 3⅛ inches in length, boasts the brilliant colors and bizarre shape of the flamboyant flower. The exception to nature's design, diamonds were added to increase the jewel's light and sparkle.

The retail cost of bijoux, though nowhere near the range of all-diamond jewelry or the more well-respected work of the Art Nouveau jewelers, paid for specialized craftsmanship and artistry. Bijoux jewelers were among the first—along with the Art Nouveau jewelers—to demonstrate the versatility of the diamond. They proved it could be matched with almost any material, be it ivory, hard stone, or watercolors, and not appear out of place. The gem bathed the artisans' handiwork with light and brought out the color and texture.

Nature themes were as important to bijoux jewelers as they had been to Art Nouveau jewelers, but the former eschewed the stylized nature of the latter for a literal rendition. Just as art critics judged the work of landscape painters Martin Johnson Heade and Frederic Edwin Church by comparing them to actual landscapes, so jewelry critics judged bijoux with a nature theme. The *Jewelers' Circular* (1892) observed, "If they [jewelers] copy flowers of any description from the most familiar ones, such as daisies and pansies, to the less frequently imitated, viz., anemones, begonias, cyclamens, mimosas, nenuphars, etc., they always reproduce the shape, even their most delicate folds and curves, but having its purpose in view to adorn the corsage of the hair, they think it more appropriate to leave color out where diamonds will look better. This is why we often see enameled flowers with diamond stamina accompanied with well-drawn leaves made of gatherings of brilliants; the stalk itself glitters. Although jewelers do not intend to improve upon nature, they evidently believe that if flowers were ever meant

The Madonna's heavenward gaze is realistically rendered in Limoges enamel. With this uncanny depiction, the anonymous enamelist was probably imitating a painting. Stained-glass windows, composed of plique-à-jour enamel and gold, are set off by a diamond and platinum frame with a gold trefoil bail, a loop at the top of the jewel used to suspend it from a necklace. The diameter of the jewel is 1½ inches.

Tiny diamonds in a platinum web, guilloche enamel, and sculpted gold borders create a pattern-on-pattern design for the Latin cross pendant measuring 1⅜ inches long. The diamond and platinum leaf bail acts as a wind stem for the watch on the reverse. A small gold plaque on the guilloche enamel interior reads "Made for Tiffany & Co. by Verger-France."

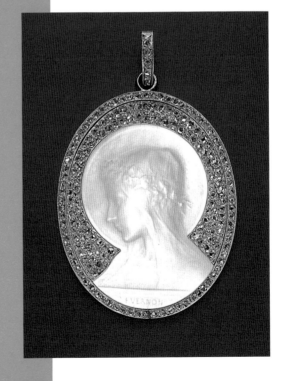

For a pendant Frédéric Vernon combined the scintillating light of diamonds set in platinum with the soft sheen of a mother-of-pearl bust of Mary. One of the best artist-jewelers in Paris, Vernon specialized in devout themes for Maison Duval and Lacloche.

to grow on corsages, skirts and shoulders, they should according to the laws of harmony which nature must obey, be slightly different in appearance from what they are in fields or gardens."

Bijoux flowers were generally composed of articulated gold petals colored by enamels with diamonds accenting the pistils and outlining the leaves. American First Lady Frances Cleveland had an impressive all-diamond daisy pin with white diamond petals and a yellow diamond center. Because the diamonds were the true colors of the daisy, the *Jewelers' Circular* (February 1887) approved of the naturalistic design: "The ornament worn by Mrs. Cleveland is indeed a 'daisy' in the popular acceptation of the word."

Tiffany created the ultimate flower bijoux for the 1889 Paris Exposition Universelle. The *Syracuse Herald* (April 7, 1889) reported on their reception in Paris: "Every one was bought up before it had been on view two days, though the price was by no means such as to put it within the reach of the multitude." Going on to reveal the name and motive of a principal buyer, the reporter impressed on readers that these orchids were not simply dress accessories but works of art. "Jay Gould, who is a great orchid lover, and whose orchid houses up in Irvington-on-the-Hudson contain the finest private collection in the world, was particularly enthusiastic over these imperishable reproductions of his favorites, and was a heavy purchaser, not meaning them for female wear, but to be kept in a cabinet for his own personal delectation." *The Jewelers Catalogue* (June 26, 1889) brashly praised Tiffany's artistry: "it beats everything shown here, and . . . surpasses in value all except the crown jewels of the effete monarchies of Europe. . . ."

The Tiffany orchids were the result of a collaboration between Edward C. Moore and Paulding Farnham. Moore presided over the Tiffany School, a studio on Prince Street in New York where designers studied texts, objects, and natural specimens to improve their draftsmanship and ability to render nature realistically. Farnham designed the Tiffany orchids after specimens culled from around the world, including Mexico, Brazil, Colombia, Guatemala, India, and the Philippines. Their subtle gradations of color were replicated exactly with matte opaque enamels made expressly by Moore with verisimilitude in mind. All that separated the Tiffany orchids from the real thing were their glittering stalks and stamens, studded with diamonds and a few other precious gems.

The themes and motifs of religious art seeped into bijoux in the form of episodes from the Bible in diamond and gold pendants and brooches that were exchanged as small mementos. Easily understood narratives conveyed messages to the faithful, and a short prayer was sometimes added in an inscription. On one diamond and gold brooch, Gabriel consoled the two Marys in front of an empty tomb. Implicit in the moment were the angel's tidings, "He is not here; for he is risen." In a turn-of-the-century context, stories of delivery served as an antidote to the fears and phobias about the modern world. Some bijoux combined the two themes, such as a gold travel medallion that depicted a scene of the prophet Elijah going to heaven in a whirlwind amid chariots of fire on one side and a prop plane, seaplane, blimp, and balloon on the other.

Among the many choices of religious iconography for bijoux, the Madonna was by far the most popular. Merciful and loving, she embodied the essential virtues people felt were in jeopardy at the turn of the century. Artisans caught her emotions, pensive, sad, and peaceful, on reliefs in the noble metals, gold and silver, as well as nonprecious materials, ivory and hard stone. Limoges enamel presented the most dramatic views of the Madonna, but this difficult technique, capable of replicating religious paintings, required a high degree of skill as well as a rare artistic talent.

Christian symbols invariably accompanied the Madonna jewels. The halo and veil, signifying dignity, sanctity, and worldly renunciation, were almost inseparable from her person. Other attributes changed according to the message: the lily stood for purity, the rose for beauty and perfection, and the color blue for its association with constancy and sorrow. A background of stained-glass windows, admirably duplicated by plique-à-jour enamel separated by a gold pattern of columns, lancet arches, foils, and lead lines, indicated Mary's connection with the church.

The diamonds in devotional bijoux can be interpreted in a few ways. In one respect, diamonds on the bails (loops to suspend jewels from necklaces) and frames were purely decorative. In another context they highlighted architectural elements. Finally, diamonds became a metaphor for the luminous beauty of holiness. A series of pendants by artisan Frédéric Vernon showed his understanding of religious symbols and his ability to convey their meaning with materials. The light-reflecting properties of diamonds packed together in the background of a Vernon pendant might very well be understood as a mandorla or an aureole radiating from the bust of the Virgin. Both symbolized the light surrounding Mary at the climax of her life, when she was taken up to Heaven.

In contrast to the Madonna jewels, rife with narrative detail, the symbol of the cross drew on historical styles for its form and decoration. Many late-nineteenth-century crosses imitated historical prototypes. Renaissance-style crosses, like the originals, had raised box settings and trailing lines of gems. For other crosses, jewelers used contemporary techniques to imitate early Christian art. By fusing small pieces of glass, or tesserae, into pictorial designs, they replicated church mosaics. Jewelers applied these micromosaics to heraldic crosses, creating a pastiche of different eras.

Transcending period styles, the simple Latin cross consisted of an upright and a transverse beam. Its symbolism as the cross of the Crucifixion made it the most common in Christian art. It was adopted by several saints whose attributes provided design motifs. Flowers represented Saint Anthony of Padua, while the lily stood for Catherine of Siena. Turn-of-the-century jewelers applied any number of designs to the Latin cross. Everything from elaborate gold work and mosaics, flower heads, and slabs of semiprecious stones, such as lapis lazuli, were adapted to the form. Because the width of the two beams was variable, watches were often mounted at the intersection.

Verger, one of the finest manufacturing jewelers in Paris, made a series of Latin cross pendants with a watch at the intersection on the reverse. The overall surface ornamentation was reminiscent of illuminated manuscripts

An ivory plaque of an animated Greek dancer echoes Léon Bakst's spirited designs for the Ballets Russes. Bold colors in the enamel and macramé tassel necklace accentuate the exoticism. Diamonds extend the range of materials, giving the jewel a suggestion of Oriental opulence.

A design by Léon Bakst dated 1910 for the Ballets Russes production of *Cleopatra* shows the fluid line and sharp colors of his costumes. Bakst's Oriental style went beyond the theater to reverberate throughout the worlds of fashion and the decorative arts, where ideas taken from his designs reappeared in other guises. From 1911 to 1929, theatrical director Serge Diaghilev and his Russian dance troupe, the Ballets Russes, transfixed Paris with modern enactments of tales like *Scheherazade, Daphnis and Chloë,* and *Narcissus.* The sounds of Igor Stravinsky that shot through modern music and the leaps of Nijinsky that energized dance were equaled by the flowing Eastern costumes of Léon Bakst.

in line, color, delicacy, proportion, and symmetry. Like the manuscripts, the Verger crosses had many sections requiring different talents from its creators. The gold was chased. The interior was a guilloche pattern: a symmetrical system of lines cut onto the gold surface by a fixed tool on an engine-turning lathe. The craftsman working the lathe needed a sure hand and a steady rhythm in order to switch gears so that the patterning of each section would dovetail. The platinum and diamond tracery composed the final element of the Verger cross. The platinum lines on top of the guilloche lines effectively added depth, in much the same way as the interlocking lines and reappearing pattern on the flat page of an illuminated manuscript. The gleam of minute diamonds mounted in platinum provided the equivalent of the white circles on medieval manuscripts offering the eye rest from the complexity of the decorated page. All of these elements enriched a pendant only 1⅜ inches high. Some of its intricacies are barely visible to the naked eye, but every aspect contributes to the overall aesthetic effect.

Bijoux jewelers revived classical and medieval imagery on ivory, miniatures, and hard-stone cameos with the same originality and flair they applied to religious themes. Each resource had the potential for storytelling; each surface had specific properties that added to the beauty of narrative. Artisans worked ivory plaques with a scrimshaw technique directly related to the one practiced by sailors on ships in the Pacific. With a sharp pointed instrument called a burin jewelers incised a drawing on the ivory surface and then rubbed the piece in cinders or filled the lines with diluted black ink. Ivory scrimshaw proved a good medium for figure drawing. The black and white lines achieved the restless movement of a dancer in motion and the result had all the spontaneity of a sketch.

A jewel dating from about 1910 containing an ivory plaque of a Greek dancer used diamonds mounted on the sides of the plaque like a curtain on a stage. They reflected light across the spirited tableau and acted as a spotlight on the small dancing figure. Other details in the design were in keeping with the exotic subject. Symmetrical lotus flowers and ivy curled around the border. The frame of the ivory plaque and the threads forming the necklace introduced color. An Eastern scheme of green and blue enamels made a scaffolding offset by two bails. Woven blue, green, and white threads formed the delicate tassel and macramé cords of the necklace. This piece exemplifies jewelry that would not have included diamonds were they not so readily available. Though carefully made, the piece employed modest materials; the presence of diamonds elevates the unpretentious design.

For a fuller narrative in color, jewelers turned to miniatures. The small watercolors allowed for background and atmospheric effects in scenes painted onto cardboard or paper. Diamonds rimmed the edges and brightened the corners of the mounts. Almost as small as grains of sand, the diamonds did not overpower the miniatures but complemented the tiny brush-strokes.

Hatot and Verger were foremost among Parisian watchmakers employing full-time miniaturists who executed works for watch faces, pendants, and brooches. Although little is known about Hatot's designers, Verger's pri-

Fernand Paillet's miniature of nymphs and cupids fishing for love in a woodland stream at sunset is signed in the lower right-hand corner, while Boucheron, the retailer for this jewel, signed the platinum and diamond fan brooch on the back. Verger, the manufacturing firm where Paillet worked, considered his miniatures a specialty of its workshop and sold them mounted in watches and brooches to retailers around the world. Brock, Spaulding, and Tiffany in America, Boucheron, Janesich, and Lacloche in Paris, Mappin and Webb in England, and W. A. Bolin in Moscow all had clients for these neoclassical jewels.

mary miniaturist, Fernand Paillet, signed his miniatures on the front and gave them titles on his worksheets. While his education and background remain obscure, Paillet emerges as a figure with artistic aspirations. His light, neoclassical episodes possess the timeless grace of wall paintings from Herculaneum and the House of the Vettii at Pompeii. They capture the winsome spirit of the carefree gods and goddesses who ate ambrosia, drank nectar, and fell in love. Shading and minute detail—blades of grass and the gentle pastel colors of a sunset—were clearly delineated on the small canvases.

When artisans engraved stories on hard-stone gems, they were following a tradition that stretched back to ancient times. Successive revivals of the art took place in the Renaissance, in the late eighteenth century after the discovery of Pompeii, and in the early nineteenth century, when a cabinet of engraved gems connoted wealth, taste, and intellect. However, the glory days of engraved gems virtually ended in 1839 with the sale of the Poniatowski collection, long considered the paradigm of an antique gem collection. The majority of its holdings turned out to be modern forgeries. Reeling from the revelation, gem engravers fell from favor. It was not until the turn of the century, when neoclassicism came back into favor, that the art of cameos and intaglios experienced a revitalization.

Diamonds played a part in the different presentation of engraved gems. Formerly they had been mounted primarily in metal, gold, silver, and silver-gilt, with few embellishing gemstones. Ostensibly this was in keeping with the simplicity of classical mounts discovered at Pompeii, but the scarcity and high cost of diamonds undoubtedly played a part. Only aristocrats, especially those at the court of Napoleon, used diamonds for their elaborate cameo suites of combs, earrings, brooches, and diadems. This all changed at the turn of the century, when engraved gems were valued as jewelry instead of collectibles. Their mounts were studded with diamonds that were readily available from South Africa.

Turn-of-the-century cameos also benefited from the painterly sensibility gem engravers brought to their material. They blended the strata of agates to achieve soft gradations of color, insinuating depth and sometimes even perspective. They also enlarged the possibilities of the medium by switching from the traditional oval to rectangular and square stones. Despite the inescapable corollary between engraved gems and classical iconography, glyptic artists expanded their horizons and looked for compositions in contemporary paintings and works on paper. One exceptional cameo replicated *The Beguiling of Merlin* by Edward Burne-Jones.

"The Beguiling of Merlin" cameo was one of the engraved gems purchased in Europe for Tiffany and brought back to New York. Although cameos had declined in favor in Europe, Americans still appreciated their history and embodiment of culture. Charles Lewis Tiffany, a founding trustee of the Metropolitan Museum of Art in New York and a devotee of antiquities, supplied his clientele with the finest bijoux as well as the finest diamonds. In the firm's workshop the cameos were mounted in gold settings with diamond frames. (It is interesting to note that the gems of Tiffany mounts were considerably larger than grains of sand, an indication of American taste for large diamonds.)

During the 1880s, when engraved gems were waning in popularity, French jeweler Germain Desbazeille brought back the art of the Renaissance portrait medal and took it one step further by mounting the gold disks in brooches and pendants. The French called these jewels *bijoux-médailles*. Initially, some were made from molds languishing in the French mint. As sales rose, new designs were produced with the reduction lathe. Mechanization made it easier for artisans to create medals, because they did not have to go through a long apprenticeship in engraving. The machinery allowed them to copy a clay bas-relief of ten to twelve inches in diameter onto a steel cylinder of a reduced scale. After a die was made from the steel model, quantities of medals were stamped. Only a superficial touching up of details was necessary in the last stage of production.

The industrial process of making *bijoux-médailles* removed it a step from the artistic world; however, many artists went into the field because it was so remunerative. Georges van der Straeten replicated his female sculptures in medals, and illustrator Jules Chéret made miniatures as well as *bijoux-médailles* versions of his posters.

B. Foisil conceived the most widely circulated *bijoux-médailles* for M. E. Martincourt in 1899. They depicted La Parisienne, the sobriquet used to describe the beautiful French women seen at café-concerts and along the avenues in Paris. Painted by Edouard Manet and Pierre-Auguste Renoir, these women were as much a part of the city as the Bois de Boulogne, Longchamp, and the Louvre, and they came to personify Paris. The diamonds on Foisil's medals of La Parisienne caused a sensation. Henri Vever stated in *La Bijouterie française au XIXe siècle*, "Its very definite fashion had much less to do with the medallion itself, pretty as it was, than with the idea the manufacturer had to set this Parisian's necklace, as well as the flowers in her hair, in rose diamonds. For a certain clientele, this addition of diamonds caused this mold, as well as other similar ones made after it, to be

An anonymous engraver transposed *The Beguiling of Merlin* to a pink and white agate cameo. His success in creating a detailed and balanced reproduction arose from his ability to reduce the scale of the painting and simultaneously transform it into a bas-relief. The bend of the knee and the outstretched book are the highlights of the carving. Despite a depth of only a few centimeters, the bower seems to extend into the distance with magical possibilities. The cameo is set in a fine diamond and gold mount signed Tiffany & Co. and engraved "L. B. A. from T. V. A. T. Apr. 30th 1884."

In Edward Burne-Jones's *The Beguiling of Merlin* (1874), the willful sorceress Vivien flourishes the book of spells she used to trap her teacher Merlin in a hawthorn bush. Sinister and sensual, the painting was popularized beyond the salons of London and Paris through photographs sold to the public. Oscar Wilde, who called the painting "brilliantly suggestive," kept a photograph of it in his study at Oxford.

preferred over productions that were sometimes of greater artistic merit."
By placing diamonds in a variety of locations, Foisil changed the emphasis
of the medal. Diamonds drew the eye up to the hair or to the neck—or to
both places.

   After World War I, the artisans responsible for bijoux disappeared
from the precious jewelry scene, and with them the artists who had enriched
the field. Precious jewelers replaced the small works of the bijoux jewelers
with items that did not require the same type of intensive specialized craftsmanship, such as small brooches with opaque semiprecious stones and
wristwatches that became the rage of the 1920s.

The imaginative lithographer Jules Chéret
painted miniatures of Parisian women for
jewelry. They were mounted with a
mother-of-pearl backing in gold and
diamond brooches by the jeweler Fonèsque
et Olive. Chéret's poster *La Dentellière*
(1900), presented at the 1900 Paris
exposition, was the inspiration for the
miniature in this brooch, 1⅛" high.
The father of the modern poster, Chéret
transformed the streets of Paris with his
bright images of women called Chérettes,
performing, working industriously, and
consuming popular products.

Bijoux-médailles incorporated diamonds as hair ornaments, earrings, necklaces, and brooches. B. Foisil used diamonds generously in a series of La Parisienne pendants (top row). E. Dropsy, on the other hand, was sparing in his application of the gem, limiting it to a necklace or a fillet, on his medals of Printemps (center row). Diamonds flicker in the shadows of the heavily modeled *bijoux-médailles* of La Parisienne by sculptor Georges van der Straeten (bottom).

CHAPTER 3

DIAMONDS AND PLATINUM

The turn of the century did not bring about the transformation in jewelry that the 1900 Paris Exposition Universelle, centering on Art Nouveau, had promised. Stylized enamel jewelry with a sprinkling of diamonds did not triumph over the Louis XV and Louis XVI motifs, which had dominated diamond designs since their inception and throughout the Art Nouveau period. These styles were so entrenched in the public consciousness that they could not be dislodged from the jewelers' repertoire. But the ideals of Art Nouveau left a mark. The intense worldwide coverage of the 1900 Paris exposition brought Art Nouveau to a wider audience than ever before and ultimately engendered a new view of diamond jewelry. The *Jewelers' Circular* (February 7, 1906) reported, "Ten or 15 years ago there was little interest felt in design. The whole thought of the jeweler was centered on making money. Art for art's sake was an unknown quantity, and as little attention was paid to the artistic qualities in design. There was not much progress made until after the last Paris Exposition. The exposition was of great benefit to jewelers. They had been asleep. It awakened and taught them to think. It taught us, among other things, to try to get away from the old conventional styles and to reach out not only for originality in design but also for artistic effects. It taught us that designs required study. That the money-value represented by a stone is not the only important thing. There was brought about a great advance in the right direction, among manufacturers and jewelers, namely, a striving more and more after artistic results."

Proper formal jewelry for royalty and society alike still had to have an array of bows, ribbons, swags, and flowers. A few exotic forms, such as an Indian frangipani flower or an Egyptian lotus, surfaced occasionally, but by and large the Versailles code of motifs held sway. What made post-1900 all-diamond jewelry different were the delicate proportions and detail carried out with the flood of small diamonds from South Africa and techniques that made platinum workable. The tried and true motifs became more refined, raising the style to a new level.

Platinum's unique properties got the kinks out of jewelry. Unlike silver, which had been the primary mounting for diamonds, platinum did not oxidize and consequently did not need gold backing to protect the skin from tarnish.

A platinum and diamond necklace by Tiffany features large diamond accents among the tiny diamonds decorating the garlands and flowers. The tiered design is characteristic of platinum and diamond necklaces of the era. It spread across the décolletage, creating a decidedly opulent look.

It kept its matte reflective surface indefinitely and was impervious to corrosion. Being much stronger than gold and silver, it could be used in much thinner and smaller elements. In addition to its merit as a mounting, platinum was the supreme enhancer of the diamond. Its bluish gray color amplified the diamond's brilliance and intensified its fire like no other metal. For the most part, small diamonds in platinum jewels were cut into circular shapes that followed the flow of curvilinear designs. Larger marquise (navette-shaped) and pear-shaped diamonds formed central and drop elements.

However, platinum's very virtues had made it difficult to exploit. Its melting point, 1772°C, was much higher than that of gold (1064°C) and almost double that of silver (961°C). Platinum could not easily be melted. Historically, jewelers had used a mouth blowpipe with an alcohol or oil lamp to melt metals. The jeweler blew into a flame with this apparatus in order to control the direction, size, and heat of the flame. Depending on the amount of oxygen his breath contained, the heat rose or fell. Because of the jewelers' inability to work platinum with traditional gold and silversmithing techniques, manufacturing had been more or less unaffected by the bluish gray metal until the scientific advances of the nineteenth century. Sometime after 1803, when English chemist W. H. Wollaston discovered a process that made platinum malleable, its potential for

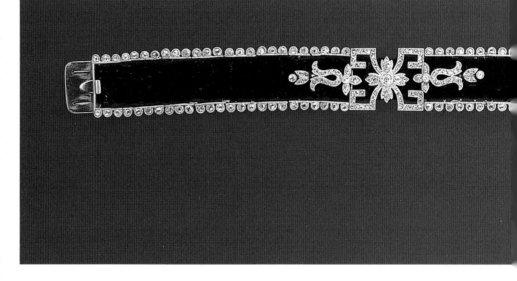

fine jewelry was investigated. It is impossible, however, to pinpoint exactly when and where, because jewelers, unlike scientists, have never been in the habit of writing reports and openly sharing their findings. In 1855, French jeweler Eugène Fontenay created one of the earliest important jewels to incorporate platinum segments into its gold mounting, a diamond blackberry diadem, illustrated in Henri Vever's *La Bijouterie française au XIXe siècle* and documented without elaboration on the use of platinum. Designed in a complex naturalistic style, the diadem was probably composed of a sheet of platinum that had been soldered on top of a gold base. The diamonds were sunk into this platinum plate. The labor-intensive process was carried out with mallets and chisels. Fontenay must have been experimenting with platinum for some time to come up with this virtuoso piece. Another significant jewel with a platinum and gold setting came from Tiffany & Co. in 1876. A show-stopper at the Philadelphia Centennial Exhibition, the peacock feather aigrette received wide media coverage for its center stone, the 30-carat Brunswick canary diamond. The platinum in the fringe part of the feather mounting went unnoticed except in trade periodicals. The *Jewelers' Circular* (March 1877) reported that it "may well be regarded as a masterpiece of diamond-setting."

Diamond and platinum garlands and stylized flowers spread across a neck velvet made by Cartier in 1906. At the center is a lozenge-shaped diamond and, suspended below it, a pear-shaped diamond in a diamond-collet frame. The fashion for diamonds set in platinum and sewn onto black velvet evolved from the nineteenth-century trend of wearing plain ribbon around the neck. Cartier purchased velvets and moiré silk for jewels from the couturier Worth, and the fashion house in turn sold the finished products. For special clients the two firms collaborated. When Worth made a gown for opera singer Lillian Nordica with a fabric lavaliere bow, Cartier embellished the tips with diamonds.

By 1886 small platinum and gold pieces were common. A watchdog of the platinum story, the *Circular* stated in 1886, "This association of gold and platinum, while by no means a new combination, is being employed with new effects on some of the more attractive jewelry." As platinum was integrated into jewelry, the *Circular* ran regular columns such as "Workshop Notes and Queries" and "Practical Notes From a Practical Man" about the intricacies of the metal.

The discovery of platinum deposits in the Ural Mountains in Russia in the 1880s gave jewelers more than enough platinum to experiment with small items such as brooches, buttons, and bracelets, using alternate links of platinum and gold. However, jewelers were unable to make anything much larger in platinum, and technology was not their only hurdle. They had

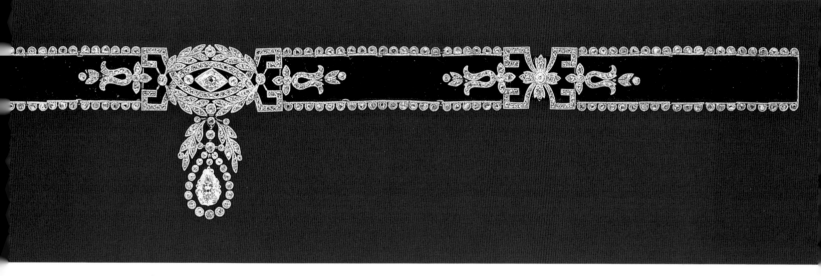

to overcome the reservations of their clients, who regarded silver as the appropriate metal for formal diamond jewelry, because of its long tradition as a favorite of kings and queens. Platinum's history as a material for cooking pots, weights, and the incandescent filament of lightbulbs added to clients' apprehension about its use in precious jewelry. Some demanded silver mountings for their diamonds even after jewelers perfected elegant platinum and diamond jewels.

Around 1900, Wilhelm Carl Heraeus, a research chemist, removed the last barrier to platinumsmithing when he discovered an effective melting process. This breakthrough freed jewelers from the tedium of shaping platinum with chisels and soldering it to gold backings. The progress in quantitative analysis had also trickled down to jewelers, who were able with this knowledge to isolate platinum from its family of metals—iridium, palladium, osmium, rhodium, ruthenium—and work out the appropriate alloy for jewelry. The standardized formula was 90 percent platinum and 10 percent iridium. (Although platinum gained acceptance around 1900, it did not receive a hallmark, a dog's head, until 1912, when the French government officially declared the ore a precious metal.)

With the mysteries of platinum's melting point and alloys solved,

Queen Alexandra of England mixed contemporary jewels with historical pieces from the British crown collection. In addition to badges, various decorations, and a draped necklace, she wears three of Queen Victoria's jewels: a diamond bar brooch at her shoulder, a diamond waterfall brooch at the plunge of her gown, and a circlet created by British crown jeweler Garrard to display the 108.93-carat Koh-i-Noor diamond. (A circlet is a circle-shaped head ornament with decorations projecting upward, usually worn tilted back and above the brow.) A gem with an extraordinary provenance, the Koh-i-Noor's string of owners can be traced back to fourteenth-century India. Alexandra's contribution to the array was her diamond and platinum collarette (an extrawide choker with a V-shaped extension dipping down to the décolletage) made by Cartier in 1904. It is a superb example of the regal treatment applied to formal jewelry at the time: the diamond-studded grillwork and fringe drape majestically across the décolletage.

jewelers, using the torch, could finally work larger sections and create all-platinum pieces. Sam W. Hoke of New York had developed and patented several torches to be used with oxygen and regular city gas. Their initial names, oxy-gas blowpipes, reflected the ancestry of the tool. The recently commercialized jewelers saw blade, which replaced the chisel, cut platinum into a multitude of dainty traceries.

Equipped with the new tools and technology, jewelers devoted their energies to experimentation within the perimeters of the inherited design repertoire. They produced endless variations on bows, ribbons, and swags, motifs that showed off the jeweler's ability to work platinum into delicate curls and swirls. Although platinum was heavier than silver or gold, it was also far stronger. The almost paper-thin settings and extraordinary surface detail did not cave in during the fabrication process, nor did it bend or break upon completion. Knife-edge platinum spokes spread their sharp edges, grillwork created webs of equidistant platinum threads, crocheted platinum radiated out in curvilinear patterns, and millegrain, small beads, covered the surfaces of jewels.

The multitude of diamonds packed into platinum mountings came in plentiful supply from the Kimberley Mines in South Africa. They had been discovered after some accidental finds by two unlikely prospectors. In 1867, a young boy found a 21-carat diamond, aptly named the Eureka. While impressive, the diamond caused little stir beyond a small group of diplomats and gemologists who debated whether the Eureka was a plant, a fluke, or a genuine find from a potential mine. The answer came loud and clear two years later, when a shepherd boy found an 83.5-carat diamond named the Star of South Africa—there must be diamonds in South Africa; the two behemoths could not be a coincidence. As soon as the news was released, miners converged on the Cape from all points of the compass, and the population rapidly boomed to over fifty thousand prospectors, all of them staking claims and hell-bent on striking it rich.

The furious mining that ensued dislodged tons of yellow earth, revealing the blue ground of a kimberlite, the matrix of the diamond. A rare igneous rock, it occurs in cylindrical "pipes" created by volcanic eruptions that took place deep in the earth thousands of years ago. The pressure of the upheaval forced a flow of gases and massive rocks to the surface. Mingled among them were octahedral crystals of pure carbon—stones otherwise known as diamonds.

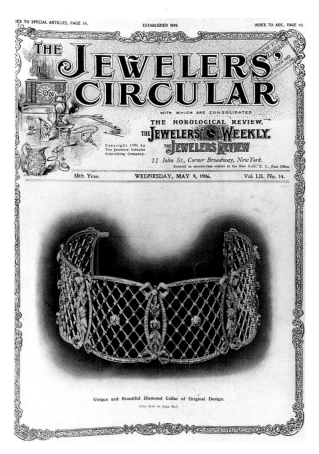

In 1906 a diamond and platinum dog collar by a Philadelphia jeweler, as meticulously crafted as Queen Alexandra's collarette, appeared on the cover of the *Jewelers' Circular*.

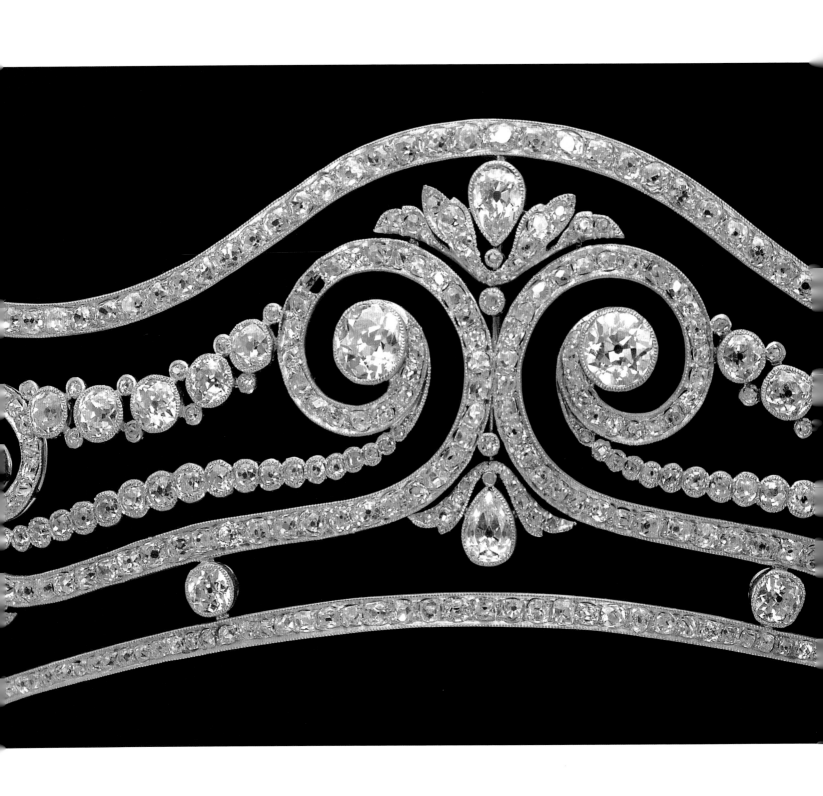

Different sizes of circular-cut diamonds set in platinum create the curvilinear pattern of this tiara by Chaumet. Pear-shaped diamonds in foliate motifs nestle among the scrolls. The close-up shows the millegrain, tiny platinum beads that are almost imperceptible from a distance. Almost all platinum jewels of the era used millegrain.

Before South Africa, only two other major sources for gem-quality diamonds existed: the Indian mines that had supplied diamonds to the ancient Romans and Western Europe, and the Brazilian mines that were discovered in 1725. Both mines, however, had virtually dried up by the nineteenth century. The South African discovery ended the prolonged drought with a flood of diamonds. So abundant were they, in fact, that prices for the coveted gem plummeted. This proved a fine turn of events for Art Nouveau jewelers and creators of bijoux, who happily studded their jewels with small diamonds, but for formal jewelers it was a mixed blessing. Diamonds lost the mystique of rarity that had always strengthened their value, and the desire to own them waned. Only after De Beers Consolidated Mines and Cecil Rhodes adroitly gained control of the mines and distribution of the gem did the passion for diamonds return, almost to the exclusion of all other precious stones.

The appetite for diamond jewelry mounted in platinum was stoked by the example of Alexandra, wife of Edward VII of England. When the couple ascended the throne in 1902, they were already veterans of the art of high living. Alexandra set the standard for jewelry and dress among the international elite. The number-one item copied from Alexandra's royal diamond jewelry

A 1909 diamond and platinum corsage ornament by Cartier showcases the Versailles motifs—flowers, ribbons, and scrolls. Large circular-cut diamonds accent the festoons. At the center is a pear-shaped diamond in a diamond-collet frame, a signature Cartier motif. During this era Cartier excelled at making magnificent tiaras and corsage ornaments, elaborate bodice decorations that were larger than a brooch and smaller than a stomacher.

Tiny round diamonds set in platinum garlands and flowers surround two pear-shaped blue diamonds of 2.66 and 2.98 carats in a delicate brooch by New York jeweler Theodore B. Starr. The matching blue diamonds, rare and extremely valuable, probably came from the South African mines that every once in a great while yielded blue diamonds in the coveted shade of sky blue. The color blue comes from an admixture of boron, a nonmetallic chemical element, in the diamond crystal.

ensemble was the tiara. Wealthy women who had no royal ties claimed the right to wear the accessory previously reserved for crowned heads. Strange as it may seem, given its reputation for formality, the tiara did not languish between formal occasions. Flexible platinum and diamond segments made it possible to alter the form, turning it into one of the most versatile of all jewels. Some could be disassembled into brooches. Still others, when flipped upside down, became flaring necklaces.

The dog collar was also popularized by Queen Alexandra, who often wore one to cover a scar. In a perfect match, the jewel finished off fashionable beaded and embroidered gowns with a wide décolletage and cinched waist. The silhouette formed a pronounced S curve that fell away in a regal court train. The dog collar echoed the cinched waist and stressed the exaggerated curves. Though the jewel had been around for some time, the updated version with garlands, grillwork, and scrolls was more intricate and detailed with the use of platinum and tiny diamonds.

The threadlike pattern of slender pieces of platinum spread across the frames of dog collars made the accessories look like elaborately woven fabric. The quality of designs brought sartorial fashion and jewelry together. Indeed, fabric was used in jewelry. Jewelers backed dog collars with black velvet, then ventured a step further by sewing platinum and diamond garlands and scrolls onto a strip of velvet. During the Second Empire plain black ribbons tied around the neck were called neck velvets. When jewelers sewed platinum and diamond motifs onto velvet ribbons the name remained the same. While capitalizing on the dog collar trend, jewelers were also picking up on the dressmakers' concept of sewing sparkling accents onto fabrics.

An even more elaborate version of the dog collar form was the diamond and platinum collarette. Depending on the extravagance of the wearer, it just touched the collarbone or dipped down and filled in a substantial portion of the décolletage. Named after an ornamental collar of lace or fur, the jewel was one of many in this era with roots in women's apparel.

Historically, the jewel with the longest association with fabric and dress was the corsage ornament, an elaborate brooch. This decoration evolved from the seventeenth-century practice of sewing diamonds set in quatrefoil mounts onto court attire and from the eighteenth-century stomacher, a V-shaped decoration of bows or flowers sewn onto the bodice. The platinum corsage ornament, albeit more delicate than its predecessors, was still large enough to cover a good portion of a woman's dress with diamonds.

These jewelry styles underwent a metamorphosis as the woman's silhouette changed around 1910. Petticoats and underskirts were reduced and the S curve gave way to a tubular shape. Paul Poiret, a one-time designer for couturier Charles Worth, is given credit for straightening the contours of dress by doing away with the corset and introducing draped gowns that fell gracefully to the floor in a columnar line.

To a certain extent, jewelry followed fashion's lead. Oversize corsage ornaments that depended on the V-shaped corset shrank, so to speak, into single elements of grillwork, lace, and bows, forming tiny, elegant brooches. Delicate draped necklaces such as the lavaliere drew attention to the vertical line. A slender slice of platinum lacework studded with diamonds meticulously crafted into an earring echoed the up-and-down silhouette. The linear direction of diamond jewelry also became apparent in headgear; the tiara yielded to the ever more youthful low-slung diadem or bandeau. Certain diadems wrapped around the crown of the hairstyle and were held by a ribbon tied at the back. Generally, these versions could also be worn as dog collars.

Within the maelstrom of changing fashions, jewelers managed a slow assimilation of motifs from foreign cultures. The exotic influences came into high relief after George V of England held a colorful durbar (a large formal assembly presided over by a British monarch) in Delhi, India, in 1911. Queen Mary, like many women, stuck with traditional nonlinear jewelry forms and the Versailles code of motifs, but others incorporated the new designs into their formal suites. Frangipani flowers, cartouches, arabesques, and geometric plaques enlivened brooches and pendants, while the aigrette, a flamboyant concoction of Oriental origin composed of sprays of gems or ostrich feathers rising from a line of diamonds, encircled the head. As different as the court favorites and the Eastern-inspired jewels may seem, they meshed harmoniously, with platinum and diamonds as the unifying features.

The style of platinum and diamond jewelry worn by nobility and the social elite from Moscow to Paris, from London to New York, was similar; there was an international consensus on precious accessories. The homogeneous quality of the style stemmed from the fact that jewelers and their clients were on the move, creating a single fashion identity for a shrinking world. The privileged of the era enjoyed stately and glamorous lives. Society traveled from country to country with ease in private railroad cars. A first-class ocean liner made crossing the Atlantic not only effortless but also diverting. Luxurious transportation made it common for New York society to mingle with nobility. Family ties linked the royalty of Russia, Germany, and England and led to international travel, shared holidays, and house parties among the court and its circle. And though the French had lost their governing nobility, there was still enough blue blood in the celebrated Paris salons to make the city a mecca for seasonal travelers.

Many large firms opened branches to follow old clients and win new ones. The importance of coronations and royal appointments drew certain

King George V poses with Queen Mary, who awed the British subjects with her flamboyant display of diamond jewelry, especially the large rocks that were cut from the 3,106-carat Cullinan diamond. On Queen Mary's head is the King George IV state diadem. Nine diamond necklaces form her collar, which suspends the Cullinan III and IV, of 94.4 and 63.6 carats, known as the Lesser Stars of Africa. Down her front, she placed three bow brooches that belonged to Queen Victoria and two platinum and diamond brooches that she commissioned from Garrard after she received several cuttings from the Cullinan. One is set with the Cullinan V of 18.8 carats and the other with the 8.8-carat Cullinan VII and the 6.8-carat Cullinan VIII. George V is covered with military medals, badges, and orders of state.

A diamond and platinum lavaliere necklace by Cartier exhibits a shift to linear designs and the influence of the Orient. Simple navette-shaped and circular connections displace garlands on the chain. A looped knot design of Eastern inspiration forms the intersection, and the elongated pendant drops display stylized patterning. With its central knot and the staggered bowlike ends, the lavaliere is another platinum and diamond jewel based on an article of clothing. Over the years its origins have been mixed up with two women. The first was a mistress of Louis XIV, Louise de la Vallière, who gave her name to the lavaliere cravat, and the second was Eve Ferroglio, who had taken Lavaliere as her stage name. The diva became associated with the diamond necklace when she was the toast of Paris, but most people still linked the style with the court lady who was the original bow lover.

jewelers into the limelight. In addition to crowned heads, any number of guests needed the proper diamond accessories. And who was better qualified to purvey the best jewelry than the king's jeweler?

The British royal family's favorite crown jeweler was Garrard. The firm had been entrusted with commissions from the royals since its 1843 appointment as crown jeweler to Queen Victoria. In this role Garrard oversaw the maintenance and preparation of state jewels. On royal occasions a senior director rode in a coach in front of the queen. After the Transvaal government gave the 3,106-carat Cullinan, the largest diamond ever discovered in South Africa—or anywhere else, for that matter—to Edward VII as a sixty-sixth birthday present in 1907, Garrard was responsible for overseeing the cutting of the gemological wonder as well as the mounting of several cleavings into crown regalia. Cullinan I, a 530.2-carat stone, went into the state scepter, and Cullinan II, a 317.4-carat stone, became the focal point of the imperial state crown. Some of the other Cullinans entered the crown collection and were set in fashionable diamond and platinum jewelry. Queen Mary commissioned Garrard around 1911 to set the Cullinan VII, an 8.8-carat cushion-cut diamond, and the Cullinan VIII, a 6.8-carat marquise-cut diamond, into a pendant brooch. It was a sign of the times that important stones were given such an artistic presentation. Platinum spokes radiated out from behind the cushion-cut diamond, which was ensconced in a platinum mount of garlands and scrolls set with tiny diamonds.

The coronation celebrations of Edward VII lasted an entire year and brought many jewelers to London to open branches. Three of the most successful were Cartier, Chaumet, and Fabergé. Everyone from Queen Alexandra to Grace Wilson Vanderbilt to the Grand Duchess Vladimir of Russia and celebrated Spanish dancer La Belle Otero shopped at Cartier. They were attracted by the fine quality of the jewels as well as the firm's keen awareness of fashion. A firm could become *the* firm if the right people crossed the threshold. Cartier was so successful at enticing the right clients that its ledgers read like the *Social Register, Burke's Peerage,* and *Who's Who* combined. At the turn of the century the three Cartier brothers, Pierre, Jacques, and Louis, covered a lot of jewelry-buying terrain for the family enterprise by going personally to different locations to obtain raw materials, service clients, and open new branches. Cartier's expansion plan that began with the opening of a branch in London for the 1902 coronation continued its outreach in 1908 with a temporary branch in Saint Petersburg, established to be close to the diamond-loving Russian royal family and aristocracy. In 1909 Cartier opened an office in New York, followed by a retail location in the former Morton Plant mansion in 1917.

Chaumet traced its history back to Nitot, Napoleon I's favorite jeweler. After two successive directors, Prosper Morel and Jean Fossin, Joseph Chaumet took over the firm in 1885 and renamed it. Like his predecessors, he was a court jeweler who made pieces with Versailles motifs for Italian, Russian, and English royalty. Chaumet, like so many other jewelers, opened a branch in London for the coronation of Edward VII and purveyed platinum and diamond jewelry to the guests.

A segment of Grace Wilson Vanderbilt's diamond and platinum plaque necklace by Cartier has a geometric frame and stylized arabesques. The motifs reflect the Eastern influence affecting jewelry design.

Jeweler to the czars, Fabergé opened a London branch in 1903, its only location outside of Russia. Celebrated for its virtuosity in enamel, culminating in the fifty-two Imperial Easter Eggs commissioned by the czars, the firm produced diamond jewelry based on the Versailles code of motifs that was equally exquisite.

Some American jewelers that did not have the tradition or the entree of the crown appointees resorted to aggressive marketing campaigns. Their platinum and diamond jewelry, however, was made in the same mode and just as beautiful as the collections of the Europeans and Russians. A pioneer of the American jewelry industry, Theodore B. Starr was a favorite of gem connoisseurs. He provided his clients with exceptional stones mounted in elegant, understated platinum and diamond jewels. When Starr died the *Jewelers' Circular* (May 15, 1907) called his firm "one of the greatest jewelry houses in the world." The work of the American jeweler Dreicer popped up in the fashion magazines as well as the routine trade periodicals. The ultra-fine platinum filaments found in Dreicer's diamond jewels were a testament to its superb platinumsmiths, a source of pride to the firm. In an advertisement the jeweler boasted, "The Dreicer flexible settings of platinum in individual designs of great merit are made by a corps of French designers on the premises." Tiffany & Co., the biggest American jeweler, with a branch in Paris dating back to the mid-nineteenth century, purveyed platinum and diamond tiaras, corsage ornaments, and tiered necklaces, a necessity for the female members of the Four Hundred, the New York social elite.

The international platinum and diamond style was not exclusive to jewelers in social capitals. The *Jewelers' Circular* (May 9, 1906) reported on a magnificent diamond and platinum dog collar made by a small Philadelphia jeweler, "Irrespective of its intrinsic value, which is considerable, a diamond collar made recently in Philadelphia, is generally regarded in the trade of that city as a notable piece of jewelry work. The scheme is especially well carried out so as to make it a lace work design, light in weight, but strong and durable. The cobwebby effect is offset and adroitly shown by contrast with a ribbonlike piece in front. Exactly 1,600 diamonds are set in the collar, which is entirely handmade of platinum and iridium and without any gold fortification whatever. On this account alone the piece would be exceptional."

While the significance of platinum and diamond jewelry is undeniable, as a style it has eluded designation. The difficulty of naming it stems from the fact that there are no single exhibitions that launched it. Most decorative arts critics around 1900 were obsessed with Art Nouveau. Those that did review diamond and platinum jewelry called it just that, unless they were referring to specific motifs by name, such as Louis XV and Louis XVI. Finally, there are no watershed dates. The style eased in around the turn of the century with the formalized trade in diamonds from South Africa and the breakthroughs in platinum technology and it eased out slowly with World War I. Of the many tags attached to platinum and diamond jewelry, Edwardian is the most prevalent. While it pinpoints the social center of the era, it overlooks the French origin of most of the designs. On the other hand,

Opposite: Grace Wilson Vanderbilt wears a collection of jewelry that her husband Cornelius Vanderbilt III purchased for her at Cartier in Paris. At the center of her bodice is a diamond rose. The brooch formerly belonged to Napoleon III's cousin Princess Mathilde, whose collection of jewelry was almost as celebrated as Empress Eugénie's during the Second Empire in Paris. To round out the regal ensemble, Vanderbilt wears an impressive diamond corsage ornament of bowknots, tassels, and fringe. Her diamond and platinum plaque necklace was commissioned from Cartier in 1908.

while Belle Epoque captures the importance of French history, it is too exclusive, since jewelers everywhere were working with the Versailles code of jewelry motifs. Moreover, the Belle Epoque time frame, late nineteenth century to 1914, is too long; among other things, the silver mountings of pre-1900 jewelry made it much bulkier than the jewelry that followed. Fin-de-siècle is also too broad a phrase to be accurate. There were other styles at the turn of the century that bore no resemblance to diamond and platinum jewels.

Because of the slowly evolving nature of the designs and technology, diamond and platinum jewelry has even been dubbed transitional. There is a kernel of truth to this slippery term. The artistry of Art Nouveau affected every level of jewelry design, and seedlings of Art Deco geometry can be found in platinum and diamond styles. But that is far from the whole story. A combination of the Versailles code of motifs and innumerable tiny diamonds set in complex and intricate platinum mountings created a style that was unto itself and never duplicated.

Queen Elisabeth of Belgium's diamond and platinum collarette-diadem by Cartier has graduated scrolls, garlands at the top border, and diamond collets around the bottom edge. The jewel could be worn as a collarette with the 5.84-carat central diamond pointing downward. It could also be worn as a diadem. In order to do so the queen attached black ribbons to the sides to extend the length of the jewel around her head. Because of the great need for variation during this era, with its profusion of formal parties and court occasions, platinum and diamond jewelry like this collarette-diadem had built-in versatility and could be worn in a number of ways.

Queen Elisabeth of
Belgium wears her Cartier
jewel as a diadem.

CHAPTER 4

DECO DIAMONDS

At the "Exposition des Arts Décoratifs et Industriels Modernes" of 1925, the French altered the course of design. Jewelers previously associated with Art Nouveau and those that had purveyed platinum and diamond jewelry styles with Louis XV and Louis XVI motifs united under one banner. Boucheron, Cartier, and Van Cleef & Arpels, crown jewelers of Europe and favorites of the rue de la Paix, joined artist jewelers Fouquet, Raymond Templier, and Vever, among others, to achieve a look free of court references and old-fashioned prototypes. Together they offered a new style characterized by geometric shapes, hard angles, and straight lines, later named Art Deco, a contraction of the exhibition title.

The geometric jewels featured semiprecious stones for color and diamonds for elegance. An integral part of the design, diamonds were more than accents. Their placement so greatly affected the patterned geometries that the designs would be incomplete without them. The brilliance of diamonds intensified the opaque color fields of coral, turquoise, jade, lapis lazuli, and black onyx. Diamonds shimmered against the translucent surfaces of nephrite and chalcedony. Arranged in a mosaic next to diamonds, iridescent mother-of-pearl broke up into many soft pastel beams of light.

Because the jewelry was so different from previous styles, it was not immediately embraced by everyone. Americans were skeptical and the British were unwilling to budge from a regal look. But the French held their course. Georges Fouquet, président du groupe des Joailliers-Bijoutiers at the exposition, rallied his fellow jewelers in an essay published in *Le Grand Negoce: Organe du commerce de luxe français* (translated by E. Gardner) in Paris in 1926, "Why should jewels not follow the natural law of evolution: music, painting, literature, all these evolve from day to day; in sciences also as in the arts. For if progress did not capture men and customs in spite of themselves we would still keep company with sedan chairs and stage coaches, nay, perhaps still be conveyed in ox wagons. Yes, the traced road must be followed. I appeal first to those designers who have exhibited: their effort must not be thrown away and there must be no retreat; next to our non exhibiting colleagues; and finally to our decorative artists, to our designers, and to our manufacturers to continue in the line in which they have begun."

Earrings by Van Cleef & Arpels feature circular-cut diamonds in a linear design connecting tiny pearls and onyx and coral drops to coral buttons.

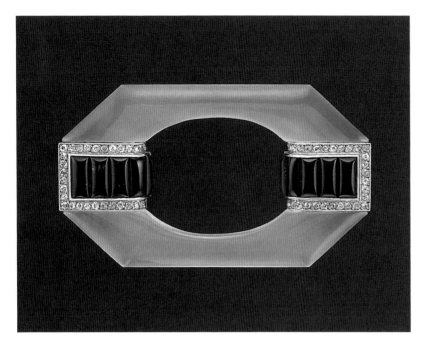

Diamonds in simple lines stand out on the octagon of the white agate and ribbed black onyx brooch by Georges Fouquet.

Fouquet took the high road, comparing jewelry to music, painting, and literature, but what really persuaded jewelers to change their approach was fashion. Clothes had evolved into a fresh young look while jewelry had remained more or less stagnant, appearing dated and dowdy with the trim new ensembles. In order to catch up, jewelers harmonized designs for the 1925 exposition with the slim, loosely structured knee-length dresses, bobbed hair, and cloche hats. Cartier, eager to prove that its jewelry meshed with fashion, abandoned the Jewelry Pavilion at the exposition altogether. Instead, the firm opted to show its collection with the couturiers in the Pavilion of Elegance.

Among the exhibits in the Pavilion of Diamonds, Pearls and Precious Stones, Boucheron's work stood out. Its jewels featured diamonds and a muted palette of carved black onyx, coral, jade, and lapis. Another rue de la Paix jeweler, Van Cleef & Arpels, a firm that had been established in 1898 and specialized in diamond pieces, came into its own at the 1925 exposition. The firm won a grand prize for a collection that included a wide bracelet with red and white roses in bloom, set with rubies and diamonds. This design, however, was exceptional; the all-diamond wide bracelet and rectangular brooch by Van Cleef & Arpels featuring geometric-shaped stones exemplified the Art Deco style. The firm also offered abstract Art Deco designs set with diamonds and semiprecious stones. Award-winning Art Nouveau jeweler Vever became an award-winning Art Deco jeweler at the exposition. The firm made shield-shaped diamond brooches and wide diamond bracelets enlivened with champlevé enamel (hollows of gold filled in with enamels), scenes inspired by the Mogul manuscripts that Henri Vever had collected.

The work of artist jewelers Georges Fouquet and Raymond Templier was stark in its shapes and color schemes. Although Fouquet had previously made ornate sinuous Art Nouveau jewels, his Art Deco pieces were distinguished by extreme minimalism. Fouquet produced jewels with black and white color schemes studded with diamonds and executed in white agate and

"A decidedly modern flapper" was the phrase *Vogue* (June 1, 1927) chose to describe stage actress Margalo Gillmore. Her short bobbed hair and sleek black dress were set off by an Art Deco diamond and crystal circle brooch pinned sideways at the front of her dress.

black onyx. Raymond Templier's work was monochromatic and rigorously geometric. He specialized in brooches that displayed expanses of highly polished platinum contrasting with large areas of pavé-set diamonds, jewels that were precursors to white Art Deco. Almost all of his repertoire consisted of these two materials in creative geometric variations. Templier's purist approach made him a leader among French jewelers.

All the jewelers at the exposition succeeded magnificently in completely changing the look of jewelry and bringing it up to date. More than simply getting women to wear their jewels, the French made them indispensable to flapper fashions. *Vogue* (June 1, 1926) reported that jewelry redeemed Chanel's little black dress: "It was this designer who originated the absolutely simple frock, a mode that demanded jewels to save it from being drab." Long, thin earrings with a pendant drop emphasized the slender silhouette. Circle brooches, fibulas, and jabot pins held a scarf in place, accented the neckline, shoulder, hip or waist, and highlighted close-fitting hats. Square-link bracelets accumulated on the arm in multiples.

Diamonds artfully combined with semiprecious stones defined the Art Deco jewels most closely related to the "Exposition des Arts Décoratifs" of 1925. However, changes were in the making. As the style won acceptance among nonexhibiting jewelers, the second wave of Art Deco exploded into a look that demanded bulk and broad surfaces. The delicate and colorful details of semiprecious stones disappeared, and a stark white palette of dia-

In a photograph taken by Edward Steichen for *Vanity Fair* (March 1931), Ziegfeld Follies girl Peggy Hopkins-Joyce flaunts an impressive collection of jewelry perfectly in keeping with the Art Deco sensibility of clean lines and geometric forms. Geometric-cut diamond rings flash on her fingers and several gem-set line bracelets and a wide diamond bracelet appear on her arm. The centerpiece of the collection is the 127-carat Portuguese diamond in a diamond choker by Black, Starr & Frost. The name attached to the diamond comes from an erroneous legend that claimed it was mined in Brazil and owned by the Portuguese prince regent. Witherbee Black had the diamond fashioned into an emerald cut, a shape developed around World War I and popular for large single diamonds in the Art Deco era. A unique feature of the Portuguese diamond is that it fluoresces blue-white beams under ultraviolet light. When Black asked if Peggy Hopkins-Joyce would sell him her $350,000 pearl necklace, she took the diamond and $23,000 in cash as payment. Like its new media-loving owner, the gem received enormous coverage.

monds cut in a wide variety of shapes took their place. It was in this era that lapidaries mastered geometric diamonds and jewelers figured out how to design with them.

American jewelers had not participated in the 1925 exposition. When the invitation arrived, Herbert Hoover, the American secretary of commerce, declined after conferring with various heads of industry. Hoover stated, "They did not consider that we could contribute sufficiently varied design of unique character or of special expression in American artistry to warrant such a participation" (Arthur J. Pulos, *American Design Ethic: A History of Industrial Design*, Cambridge, Mass., 1986, p. 304). Instead, the Americans formed a commission to visit and analyze the work displayed at the exposition.

When the style switched to an all-white diamond mode, the American jewelers joined the French in purveying Art Deco jewelry. They knew the gemmy look would appeal to their clients, who had an appetite for diamonds. Two American firms with high visibility, Black, Starr & Frost and J. E. Caldwell, took out lavish full-page advertisements in *Vogue* on a monthly basis. Black, Starr & Frost, founded in 1810, had been known as the Diamond Palace of Broadway. During the twenties, Witherbee Black, a descendant of co-founder William Black, helped maintain the firm's preeminence. In 1929

Opposite left: Joan Crawford's diamond bracelet by Raymond C. Yard shows adroit positioning of baguette, epaulette, and marquise shapes on three pavé-set diamond panels. Marquise-cut diamonds form a gently scalloped border.

Opposite right: At the Coconut Grove nightclub in Hollywood Joan Crawford is flanked by bandleader Guy Lombardo (on the left) and husband number-two, Franchot Tone (on the right). A pair of wide diamond bracelets shine on her wrist. The one on the top is her Yard jewel.

it merged with an equally venerable firm of silversmiths, the Gorham company, founded in Providence, Rhode Island. They presented their merger as that of "Two of the oldest and most famous Fifth Avenue Houses." The Chestnut Street Philadelphia jeweler J. E. Caldwell, founded in 1830 by James Emmett Caldwell, became internationally known during the twenties with all-white jewels that featured arrangements of geometric diamonds, the firm's favorite stone. The copy for a December 1928 advertisement read, "The Diamond, more than any other jewel, has ever been the gift of happiest portent. In ancient belief, it assured peace and happiness."

Raymond C. Yard's understated approach contrasted with the high profile of Black, Starr & Frost and J. E. Caldwell. Raymond C. Yard established the firm that bears his name in 1922 at the age of thirty-seven and rapidly became one of the best Art Deco jewelers in America. But only those who had seen or owned Yard jewels knew it, since Yard never advertised. This discretion endeared the firm and its founder to conservative East Coast families and some Hollywood movie stars like Joan Crawford who found their way to the exclusive salon.

White Art Deco diamond jewelry featured a multitude of geometric diamond shapes, some of which were new to jewelry. And if they were not new, they were employed in new ways, a change spelled out in a 1929 advertisement by Black, Starr & Frost: "Modernism in jewelry today demands that precious stones be cut with sharp angles and long slim facets. And, certainly, these new cuttings . . . the baguette, the trapeze, the parallelogram, the triangle, and the half-moon . . . reveal a hitherto undiscovered beauty in the diamond."

The baguette-cut diamond got its name from the shape of the eponymous French bread. Originally, the shape had rounded corners, because lapidaries were unable to cut right angles in diamonds. They had achieved the geometric baguette with softer precious stones—rubies, sapphires, and emeralds—but the diamond, the hardest substance known to man, eluded them. Then, in the mid-teens, lapidaries figured out how to true the sides and create rectangular-shaped tables surrounded by four step-cut facets in the shape of isosceles trapezoids. The baguette rocketed to the forefront of jewelers' materials. Its bricklike forms became the structural components of the flaring elements and perpendicular motifs that constituted the heart of Art Deco jewelry.

A variety of circular cuts with different facet arrangements appeared in pavé settings, the backdrop for all the fancy work with diamonds. Literally "paving" with gems, the pavé setting spread circular-cut diamonds across the surface of a jewel. The most basic circular cut was the single cut of sixteen facets, usually weighing under 0.05 carats. The light emanating from the cut did not match the intensity of diamonds with more facets. Nevertheless, the less expensive single cuts appeared in Art Deco wide bracelets, which called for large quantities of gems for effect. One circular-cut diamond employed in Art Deco pavé settings, the old European, came cheaply since the diamonds were extracted from unfashionable antique pieces. The earliest version of the modern brilliant, the old European had a small table and a heavy crown.

Another early form of the modern brilliant was the Mazarin cut. The gem received its name because Cardinal Mazarin supposedly presided over the development of the shape in 1615. (Not one of the famous diamonds bequeathed by the cardinal to Louis XIV was a Mazarin cut.) The shape had sixteen facets above the cushion-shaped girdle and sixteen below. Because of the equal number of facets at the top and bottom, the Mazarin cut was also referred to as the double cut.

The next breakthrough leading to the modern brilliant coincided with the flood of diamonds from Brazil. In the early eighteenth century Peruzzi, a Venetian lapidary, designed a circular cut with fifty-eight facets (the same number found in the modern brilliant). The eighteenth-century shape, named brilliant, reflected more light than previous shapes. And it was the most popular until 1919, when twenty-one-year-old engineer Marcel Tolkowsky designed the modern brilliant on paper and published it in *Diamond Design*. Tolkowsky had mathematically worked out a new set of measurements for the fifty-eight facets, shortened the depth (the length of the diamond from the table to the culet), and smoothed the girdle to make it completely round. The great advantage of the pattern lay in the redirection of light through the top of the stone. Light could not escape through the bottom, or pavilion, of the modern brilliant, as it had in the older versions. It

Lily Damita's diamond bracelets, packed with a multitude of old-European- and single-cut diamonds, were designed to be conspicuous. For more flash, even larger old-European-cut diamonds were added as accents. The wide bracelet above has three old-European-cut diamonds punctuating the design, and the link watch bracelet below features a 2.5-carat old-European-cut diamond at the center. The gem-set panel opens to reveal the watch face.

Hollywood actress Lily Damita, wife of the swashbuckling star Errol Flynn, wore five diamond bracelets in a fashion portrait for *Vanity Fair* (January 1, 1931) by George Hoyningen-Huene. Her wide bracelet and link watch bracelet are second and third from the right. During the Art Deco era it was not unusual for women to wear five or six diamond bracelets at a time.

In a fashion spread for *Vogue* (November 10, 1930) comedienne and author Ilka Chase, daughter of *Vogue*'s editor-in-chief Edna Woolman Chase, models a diamond choker and double diamond clips by Van Cleef & Arpels on either side of the neckline of her Jean Patou dress. The most functional jewel of the Art Deco era, the double clip could be worn as one jewel or divided into two parts: pinned on either side of an open neckline, they made symmetrical accents; pinned one on top of another they composed an asymmetrical point of interest. Clip brooches accentuated the décolletage, the hip, or the plunge at the back of a gown. They were also attached to evening bags and hats.

bounced back through the crown, maximizing the dispersion (the separation of white light into spectral colors) and its brilliance (the intensity of the reflection of light from its crown). The impressive modern brilliant brought more "life"—dispersion, brilliance, and scintillation (the flashes of light emitted from the diamond when the wearer moves)—to diamonds than ever before. The look of the modern brilliant further widened the gap between prewar and Art Deco jewelry.

A small percentage of diamonds come from a rough that is not a perfect octahedron and so cannot be made into circular brilliant cuts. Instead, these benefit from the marquise cut, an elongated version of the brilliant with a boat-shaped girdle and points at both ends, developed in France in the 1740s. Its name has been attributed to both Louis XV's mistress, the marquise de Pompadour, and the rings with a marquise-shaped decoration worn by Louis XV's courtiers as a sign of their rank. The *Jewelers' Circular* (February 21, 1929) reported on the use of the gem in Art Deco pieces: "Grouped marquise-cut gems give an unusual amount of light and faille to a jewel. Used separately they become at once the point of interest in the design. Ranged in a row they outweigh in attraction any central plaque of gems with which a piece may be adorned. Of all gem cuttings, the marquise shape is perhaps the most difficult to blend with other gem forms, but rightly handled it gives a jewel enviable distinction."

Other shapes fashioned from unusual diamond rough and found in Art Deco jewelry included square and emerald cuts. The square-cut diamond has a square table and four step-cut facets (isosceles trapezoids). The emerald, a square or rectangular-shaped stone fashioned from a long rough, has numerous step-cut facets on the crown and pavilion with chamfered (diagonally cut) corners. The long facets of the gem do not bring out the same brilliance as the circular modern brilliant cut, but the shape was popular for the extraordinary elegance of its long lines. The emerald cut received its name because it was mostly applied to emeralds. Emerald-cut diamonds as well as square, marquise, triangles (a three-sided step cut), and half moons (essentially a brilliant sliced in half) were classified as fancy cuts.

The glamour of all-diamond Art Deco jewelry kept pace with the new glamour of fashion. The stock-market crash in 1929 and the ensuing economic depression saw the passing of the flapper; her short skirts gave way to a longer hemline and a graceful, flowing silhouette. For the fashionable, the sophisticated colors narrowed to black and white, extremely flattering backdrops for diamond jewelry. With white ensembles, the diamonds provided a seamless effect with areas of intense sparkle, whereas with black dresses, diamonds shone as powerful highlights.

The bold forms of white Art Deco jewelry were influenced by architecture, the most visible aspect of the postwar recovery. Americans viewed skyscrapers as symbols of progress, especially the Empire State Building in New York, at the time the tallest building in the world. In Europe, Le Corbusier, Walter Gropius, and Ludwig Mies van der Rohe transformed architecture with a philosophy of simplicity that rejected applied ornamentation and instead emphasized proportions and the disposition of shapes. As the *Jewelers' Circular* (February 23, 1928) analyzed it in "The Tendency of Art and Industry," "From architecture to jewelry seems a long step, but the apparent space is easily covered by the same characteristics: simplicity, directness of purpose, appropriateness, liveliness, originality."

Some jewels offered obvious translations of architecture into jewelry. In diamond "temple of love" brooches, geometric-shaped diamonds formed the tiny building blocks that gave the designs integrity. Baguette and square-cut diamonds made up the steps and columns, and half-moon-cut diamonds supplied the domes. Although Greek temples usually heralded revivals, here their venerated forms had inspired architects and jewelers who prided themselves on modernism. Cartier created a series of little "temple of love" brooches that were built up with baguettes, squares, and one half-moon-cut diamond for the dome. Black, Starr & Frost created two elaborate "temple of love" brooches with double baguette-cut diamond doors opening to reveal a small picture frame.

In the abstract, architectural elements appeared everywhere in white Art Deco jewelry. Double clip brooches imitated cartouche elements on top

When decorator Elsie de Wolfe (Lady Mendl) returned to New York from Paris in 1925 on the S.S. *France*, she wore a diamond "temple of love" brooch by Cartier on her hat. One of the first architectural baguette-cut diamond designs, the jewel was illustrated in *Vogue* (November 15, 1927) and described as "one of the 'Temple d' Amour' pins that have struck such a distinctive note in modern jewellery."

A "temple of love" brooch by Cartier translates architectural features into diamonds with a half-moon-cut diamond and a small square-cut diamond as its dome. Multiple sizes of diamonds in baguette and square cuts form the entablature, columns, and pedestal.

The facades of both temple of love brooches by Black, Starr & Frost-Gorham are defined by baguette-cut diamonds set vertically on the doors and three additional baguettes that accent the doorposts and the keystones. Circular-cut diamonds cover the cornices and domes. Gems in colorful arcs above the doors communicate a hidden message. The first letter of each gem—diamond, emerald, amethyst, ruby, emerald, sapphire, topaz—spell "dearest." The diamond doors of both brooches open to reveal a picture frame. The image in the brooch on the right shows Witherbee Black of Black, Starr & Frost-Gorham, who gave the jewel to his wife Ethel as a Christmas present in 1930.

Washington socialite Evalyn Walsh McLean flaunts several wide diamond bracelets and a diamond panel necklace. Suspended from a diamond chain is the famous 44.5-carat Hope diamond. In 1669, Jean-Baptiste Tavernier sold the fabulous blue diamond from the Indian mines to Louis XIV. The gem's inky blue color was indicative of the Kollur mines in the Golconda region of India. Louis XIV enjoyed wearing it plainly in his cravat pin. His successor, Louis XV, had it remounted in a magnificent gem-set Golden Fleece decoration. After it was stolen from the French treasury in 1792, the recut diamond turned up in London, where the Hope family, the source of its name, bought the gem. The Hopes held on to the gem for a couple of generations before it hit the open market. Cartier-Paris purchased the diamond and sold it to McLean around 1912. Like many diamonds with a long history, the Hope carried a fatal curse; misfortune and death supposedly stalked its owners. Undaunted, McLean had the Hope diamond blessed by a monsignor and wore it in good health all her life.

of entryways. When separated into two parts, double clip brooches looked like sconces or decorative motifs on the spaces between stories of buildings and at their corners. Earrings and light fixtures had a remarkable affinity. Girandole earrings, descended from their seventeenth-century prototypes,

resembled miniature chandeliers with three pear-shaped diamond drops. A streamlined version of the original Baroque design, Art Deco girandoles were composed of baguette and circular-cut diamonds. Long drop earrings, differentiated from pendant earrings by their slender form, approximated the interior lighting of modern buildings. The jewels had hanging rods suspending a wider element.

Bracelets suggested the aggressive perpendiculars, horizontals, symmetrical curves, and step patterns of skyscrapers. The solid, plain perpendicular or plinth slicing the facade of a building corresponded to a straight-line bracelet made up of a single row of gems. Diamond straight-line bracelets usually consisted of baguette or square shapes. Diamond link bracelets corresponded to the fenestration of buildings, the up-and-down lines of solid masonry alternating with windows. In general, circular-cut diamonds were set in the links and baguettes formed the connectives. Wide bracelets embodied the architectural spirit of the age. Solid lines, open spaces, unbroken masses, and recesses were a few of the details transcribed from buildings and laid out on repetitive panels. The finest wide bracelets incorporated a multitude of diamond shapes fit together like a jigsaw puzzle of gems. Art Deco bracelets were a passion for Raymond C. Yard, who, like many jewelers, felt the highest artistry in precious jewelry design resided in the matching and arranging of different diamond shapes.

A drastic departure from previous styles, Art Deco introduced geometric and modern architectural forms to jewelry. The style made such an impact that almost all twentieth-century jewelers from the twenties on either operated from its premise or reacted against its rigorous hard-edge principles.

CHAPTER 5

DIAMOND NATURALISM

The rosebud bracelet by Flato—with its rose theme, all-diamond fabrication, and graceful, feminine lines—reflects a forward vision as well as a deference to the antique. The tendrils and buds, set with brilliant-cut diamonds, twine over and under the branch like a luxuriant rambler. Small, slender baguettes mounted on the curving branch form the central axis and allow for a highly flexible mount; each articulated segment is set with three baguettes. Old-fashioned rose-cut diamonds dot the design. The seventeenth-century diamond shape has a flat base and twenty-four facets that come to a point on top like a rosebud. Flato's use of the rose cut provided texture and points of interest. The rose cuts were also a clever pun on the rose motif of the jewel.

During the early 1930s, the hunky architectonic features of white Art Deco jewelry maintained their mass appeal. There were those, however, who longed for a softer look in their diamond jewelry. Naturalism, and the grace and femininity that characterized its curvilinear forms, came as a refreshing alternative. Jewels ranging from diamond-encrusted rose bracelets to seashell brooches with just a splash of the gem appeared on the market. At the same time, an interest in antique jewelry resurged. This coincidence, a desire for something new and a respect for the old, accounted for the breadth of naturalistic designs in diamond jewelry.

One of the first to participate in the drama of changing styles was Chanel. The designer had endorsed costume jewelry in the twenties, when precious Art Deco was the rage, but she did an about-face in the flat economy of the early thirties, designing a collection of diamond jewelry. According to *Vogue* (February 1, 1933), "Now, her [Chanel's] interest is in real jewels—in genuine diamonds—for it is her contention that the *crise* has set afoot a craving for authenticity." In fact, she said, "I chose the diamond because it represents the highest value in the smallest volume." Chanel put the collection on exhibit, opening first in Paris in 1932 in the designer's town house in the rue du Faubourg-Saint-Honoré, and then in New York in 1933, displaying such prewar motifs as comets, bows, and feathers—a far cry from the clean, abstract lines of Art Deco. Chock full of antique-cut diamonds, the oversize hair ornaments, necklaces, and décolletage pins paid tribute to past styles.

A prelude to naturalism, Chanel's revivalist jewels caused people to look at old designs in new ways. *Vogue* (February 1, 1933) spelled out her goal: "For Chanel only asks to be copied in this idea—she doesn't sell jewels—she has no desire to compete with jewelers." She wanted to move her clients on to something new. Finding in diamonds the clearest symbol of the romantic direction Chanel wished fashion to take, she used luxurious diamond jewelry as her lure.

Like Chanel, jewelers were reassessing the beauty of old designs, but under slightly different circumstances. During the Depression, families suffering fallout from the stock-market crash sold important heirlooms from

PRINCESSE JEAN-LOUIS DE FAUCIGNY-LUCINGE, MADAME BALLI, AND BARON DE GUNZBURG AT THE EXHIBITION

ALL THAT GLITTERS

SO long as Mademoiselle Gabrielle Chanel has a hand in this entertaining business of fashion, you can always expect something unexpected to happen. Once again, she has set Paris and New York humming with an idea of hers—not this time in the field of clothes, where she primarily operates, but in the realm of jewels!

Not "phony" jewels, either, such as the glass baubles she flung to the world back in the days when there was money to burn—baubles that she believed in then because they were "without arrogance in a period of too easy *luxe*." Now, her interest is in real jewels—in genuine diamonds—for it is her contention that the *crise* has set afoot a craving for authenticity. And her exhibition of diamond ornaments in Paris (and now in New York) is just another evidence that the Chanel creative streak goes on burning with hat-lifting ardour.

Upsetting the well-known apple-cart, Mademoiselle Chanel uses nothing but the old-fashioned, pre-War, brilliant cut diamonds in this mammoth array of ornaments . . . and sets them (upsettingly enough) in the crudest sort of settings. So crudely are they set, indeed, that they are more like stage jewellery than anything else; as some one put it, they are "the imitation of the false." Oddly enough, or maybe not so oddly, these real stones set like false ones have a very dramatic, 1933 spirit; and, aside from the ideas they may give you for having your old stones reset, they will perhaps give women the courage to wear false ones

in the various ways she has suggested. For Chanel only asks to be copied in this idea—she doesn't sell jewels—she has no desire to compete with jewellers.

Surely, the enchanting hair ornaments are going to start many of us putting things in our hair again. That lovely feather made of diamonds (that's it below) is worn like a bandeau pushed far back from the brow. Another hair ornament is like a sheaf of diamond wheat tied in the centre and held on the head by an invisible band that goes under the hair. Stars and comets, and stars mounted on crescents, are others that appear both as hair and hat ornaments.

The constellations seem to be Mademoiselle Chanel's great inspiration, and her comet necklace—a star nestling against the neck at one side with trailing strands of diamonds coming round the back and falling in a shower down the other side (eyes on the opposite page) is not only amusing, but does away with clasps—one of Chanel's pet hates. Then there are enormous diamond sunbursts—especially one of yellow diamonds set in gold—intended either as a hat ornament or brooch to fasten a fur cape or neckpiece; amusing diamond stars and bow-knots for the same purpose; star ear-rings; and all sorts of necklaces and bracelets that come apart and become other nice ornaments.

But the manner in which this exhibition was presented in Chanel's own house, which is one of the most beautiful in Paris, was almost as interesting as the exhibition. Charity and the diamond industry were both benefactors. The beautiful white-and-gold drawing-rooms were cleared of furniture, dimly lighted by Wendel with ingeniously concealed spot-lights, which fell on the objects, which, for the most part, were protected by square glass cases resting on columns. In each of these cases was a wax figure, exquisitely coiffed and made up, on which were shown the jewels as they were intended to be worn. On entering, one got the impression of a museum of statuary in which these busts were presented with fairy-like radiance.

A FRINGE NECKLACE AND A FEATHER HAIR-ORNAMENT

ANDRÉ KERTÉSZ

---

their collections. Firms that had made their reputations on contemporary work bought up these antique pieces and integrated them into their advertising and publicity campaigns. American jeweler Trabert & Hoeffer offered the diamond earrings of the Russian empress Catherine the Great. In an advertisement for the jewels, R. J. Trabert himself wrote an essay entitled "The Story of These Resplendent Historical Earrings." A roundup of magnificent jewelry in a *Town & Country* (November 1937) article, "These Disarming Women Ablaze," listed some historical pieces and where they could be purchased. Black, Starr & Frost, for one, had diamond and pearl earrings that had belonged to Empress Carlota of Mexico. Cartier offered an all-diamond Russian imperial nuptial crown worn by royal brides. American jeweler Paul Flato sold a piece from the collection of the Diamonds of the Crown of France, Empress Eugénie's currant-leaf diamond brooch, to the box holders of the Metropolitan Opera as a gift for retiring diva Lucrezia Bori. The consistent media coverage of antique jewels revealed the role they had played in history; it was an education that gave the public an appreciation for their salient characteristics of femininity and grace, two traits notably lacking in Art Deco work.

The taste for the antique that permeated jewelers' inventories and the fashion magazines was brought to a larger audience by Hollywood movies and movie stars. Mae West gave the old-fashioned look an electric shock in her first film, *Night after Night* (1932). After a hatcheck girl gushes, "Goodness, what beautiful diamonds," referring to West's antique array, the actress replies, "Goodness had nothing to do with it." In the historical dramas churned out by Hollywood during the thirties, jewelry played an important

A double-page layout from *Vogue* (February 1, 1933) shows Chanel's diamond jewelry exhibition. The old mine-cut diamonds and prewar motifs Chanel chose lent the jewels an antique look, signaling a return to feminine jewelry.

part. Generally it was fake, but on occasion filmmakers managed to get their hands on the real thing. For the period film *Conquest* (1937), Trabert & Hoeffer, Inc.- Mauboussin furnished Greta Garbo with the gem-set necklace purported to be the jewel Napoleon had given Empress Marie-Louise at their son's birth. Some actresses who had their own antique jewelry wore them in their movies, even when the setting was modern. The jewels meshed seamlessly with contemporary styles that had also taken a revivalist tack, with long, fuller skirts and off-the-shoulder dresses coming into favor. In the screwball comedy *The Divorce of Lady X* (1938), Merle Oberon flaunted her Second Empire necklace that had belonged to the wife of Baron Haussmann, the city planner responsible for the reorganization of Paris. A baroness's necklace, or any other grand antique jewel, for that matter, enhanced the image of screen royalty that actresses and studios desired to project during the glamour years of Hollywood.

Real blue bloods dusted off and polished their historical jewels at the coronation of George VI and his consort Elizabeth of England in 1937. The crown jewels they wore symbolized the continuity of the monarchy that had appeared shaky after the abdication of Edward VIII. Elizabeth wore jewels from the collections of Queen Victoria and Queen Alexandra during the festivities, and pictures of them appeared in newspapers and magazines. The pageantry powerfully reinforced the eternal glamour of diamond regalia.

In all, antique jewelry that had been viewed as dowdy, outdated paraphernalia during the Art Deco era had made a comeback. The combination of Chanel's exhibition, precious jewelry advertising, publicity, the stamp of approval from Hollywood, and the coronation in England established it as chic. However, magnificent items of celebrated provenance posed a supply problem: they were a finite commodity.

Formal houses such as Cartier and Raymond C. Yard filled the void with modern pieces inspired by what they admired in the old. Studying period jewels and riffling through their archives, fine jewelers pondered how turn-of-the-century designs could be reworked. They eliminated details, such as swags, ribbons, and garlands, that seemed finicky and old-fashioned. Instead, they focused on flowers whose lines were fluid and feminine and foliage that could wrap luxuriantly around the neck or wrist.

The diamond was the first choice among gems for these naturalistic jewels because it linked the pieces with antique jewelry, their source of inspiration. Jewelers used diamonds the same way they had been used at the turn of the century, in abundance and to the exclusion of all other gems. Jewelers also returned to the circular cut as their principal diamond shape. But this time around they applied the brighter brilliant cut to undulating surfaces as well as rounded contours. Its circular shape snugly fit the crevices and curlicues of vines and blossoms. The baguette, the most popular Art Deco diamond shape, was relegated to subsidiary areas requiring straight or curving lines, such as the stems and veins of leaves, flowers, and ribbons. The two cuts made syncopated patterns of smooth and twinkling light on the jewel's surface.

A section of Empress Eugénie's 1855 currant-leaf bodice decoration sold at the auction of the Diamonds of the Crown of France in 1887 reappeared on the market during the thirties when historical styles won renewed interest. The jewel is distinguished by its beautiful design, large size—approximately 5 inches in length—and the big diamonds studding the aiguillettes and the large diamond center stone. Originally mounted in silver and gold, the jewel was dipped in a platinum-based wash in the thirties. It was a common practice at the time to give the silver mountings of antique jewels a platinum finish. Though antique jewels had returned to fashion, in general women preferred platinum mountings for their formal diamond wear.

In marked contrast to flat and linear Art Deco, nature-theme jewelry had sculptural, almost three-dimensional platinum mounts. The volume of these gem-set jewels was a characteristic feature of the thirties nature jewelry from formal houses, exemplified by Merle Oberon's rose brooch by Cartier and Queen Nazli of Egypt's rose diamond suite by an anonymous jeweler. Both jewels had diamonds set with their pavilions pointing inward, sideways, and downward in tiers. The voluminous mountings gave the roses the semblance of unfurling their petals.

Formal establishments added drama to their nature jewels with magnificent diamond settings, while other jewelers, such as Flato and Boivin, made the style an opportunity for design innovation. They captured nature's organic and sometimes unruly growth in ways that were gutsier and more adventurous than those of other jewelers. Both Flato and Boivin had their own

Berthaud's photograph for the auction catalogue of the Diamonds of the Crown of France shows the numerous segments broken down from Empress Eugénie's currant-leaf bodice decoration. Though they were only segments, the number and size of diamonds in each one was extraordinary.

At an NBC studio appearance, Metropolitan opera star Lucrezia Bori wears a currant-leaf brooch that once belonged to Empress Eugénie. The jewel was presented to Bori by Mrs. Vincent Astor on behalf of the Metropolitan Opera box holders at the soprano's final performance. As she was one of the most beloved opera stars, it was an emotional evening. In her obituary (May 15, 1960), the *New York Times* recalled the event: "Miss Bori's popularity, as much as her artistry, made her farewell appearance at the Metropolitan on March 29, 1936, one of the most moving experiences of that theatre. The audience cheered and stood for twenty minutes in homage. Women wept as they waved scarves and hand-kerchiefs and men stamped as she appeared for the last time before the golden curtain." Not simply a great talent, Bori had pitched in to raise desperately needed funds for the Met during the Depression. After she retired, she became the first singer to serve on the Metropolitan's board and for a time she was chairman of the Metropolitan Opera Guild. Near the end of her life, Bori returned the currant-leaf brooch to the Metropolitan Opera in her bequest, where it is on display during the opera season.

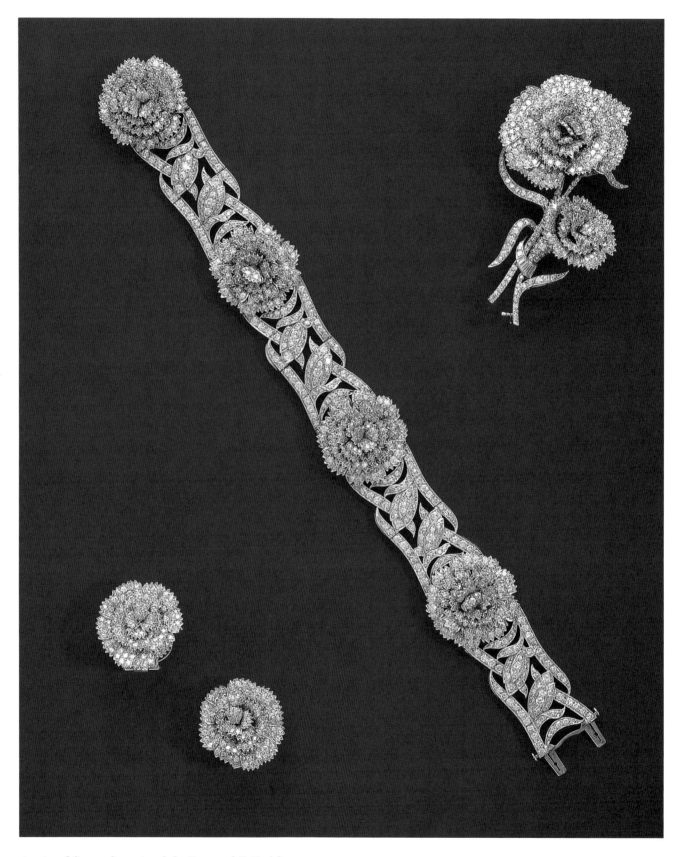

A suite of diamond rose jewels by Raymond C. Yard features an
abundance of tiny diamonds, evocative of turn-of-the-century
platinum and diamond jewelry. The size of the gems gives the jewels
an exceptionally delicate appearance.

This diamond and platinum rose brooch by Cartier is the largest of a set of three owned by Merle Oberon. The clusters of petals center on pistils that are set *en tremblant*. The setting of stiff projecting small wire springs terminating in diamond-set motifs that quiver with the movements of the wearer originated in the eighteenth century. The animated mechanism was originally designed to make diamonds shimmer in flickering candlelight.

Two of Merle Oberon's Cartier diamond rose brooches appear in her hair at a formal gala. These roses are in the form of the rose of Picardy, a dramatic flower that blooms and dies in a single day. Oberon continued to wear the roses during her third marriage to an industrialist who developed the Mexican resort Acapulco. Whenever she entered a nightclub in Mexico, the mariachi players struck up the song "The Rose of Picardy." The roses had become symbolic of Oberon's dramatic beauty.

Merle Oberon wears three diamond rose brooches by Cartier at the top of the slot seams on her Orry-Kelly suit. The jewels, a wedding present from her husband, director Alexander Korda, were sentimental favorites. She matched them with a couple of costumes in the tearjerker *'Til We Meet Again* (1940). In one scene, she wore them on a neck velvet and in another on her suit. A press release from the period said Oberon assisted in "the campaign to wear diamonds outdoors and in the daytime . . . with good taste."

ideologies about jewelry and diamonds, which came through in their work.

Although it became fashionable in some circles during the late thirties to use semiprecious and unusual stones and denigrate diamonds, Flato remained loyal to the gem, working with diamonds more than any other stone. Before Harry Winston became the most important retailer of diamond jewelry in the world, he was a wholesaler dealing in loose diamonds, and Paul Flato was his number-one customer. Flato reminisced, "One night, my telephone rang at four o'clock in the morning and an operator said, 'Brazil calling,' followed by an elated Winston, 'This is Harry, Paul. I just bought a diamond mine—you have to sell a lot of diamonds.'" After Winston's bonanza, Flato said, "My clients began to wear a lot of diamond jewelry."

With Adolph Kleaty, his head designer, carrying out the ideas on paper, Flato created an extensive collection of diamond jewelry. Extraordinarily extravagant nature-theme diamond jewelry set in platinum was the firm's specialty. Not content to make a simple rose brooch, by the time Flato finished a session with Kleaty it had turned into a rambler that twined around the wrist on a baguette-cut diamond stem sprouting rose-cut diamond buds. The antique designs Flato bought and sold fueled his creativity. Taking a detail from an old jewel, he would rework it and come up with something totally new. From Empress Eugénie's currant-leaf brooch, Flato took the single leaf motif and created a collection of currant-leaf jewelry in necklaces, bracelets, rings, and brooches. Flato did not let the high intrinsic value of diamonds keep him from expressing his distinctive brand of playfulness. One of his most unusual designs was a fully three-dimensional double apple pavé-set diamond bracelet. The wit apparent in Flato's diamond jewelry designs also shone through in the advertising campaign he wrote himself. In one ad he teased his clients about their competitive nature: "It is indeed gratifying to have your dearest friend *or* fondest enemy rush up, exclaiming 'Darling! Where did you get that *perfectly marvelous, amazing* new clip?' And it is even more gratifying to be able to answer. 'Oh, my dear, it's one of Paul Flato's new designs!'"

Flato's cowboy attitude toward precious jewelry reflected his background. He was born in 1900 in Flatonia, Texas, a ranching town named after his great-grandfather. In this unlikely place he discovered his calling. "My first love of jewels," Flato confessed, "came from watching the gypsies who camped near us in Texas tinkering and making jewels—never dreaming I too would be a tinker one day. I was ten years old and would watch for hours." A scant eighteen years later, Paul Flato owned an upstairs jewelry salon at 1 East Fifty-seventh Street in New York. In 1938 Flato added a branch in Los Angeles at 8637 Sunset Boulevard, opposite the Trocadero nightclub. Constance Collier, stately lady of the silver screen, was a sponsor of the shop and acted as a magnet to attract her movie star friends, young and old. Some stellar personalities who shopped at Flato in Los Angeles included screen goddesses Marlene Dietrich, Ginger Rogers, Joan Bennett—to say nothing of gossip columnist Hedda Hopper, opera star Lily Pons, dancer Irene Castle, comedienne Fanny Brice, performer Carmen Miranda, bandleader Eddy

A world-class jewelry collector, Queen Nazli commissioned this suite of rose jewelry from an anonymous jeweler in the thirties. The gargantuan diamond-set petals in the necklace and earrings unfurl on multiple levels. Baguette accents and a barrel-shaped clasp, carryovers from Art Deco design, enhance the collar of the necklace.

Charlie Chaplin dances with his wife Paulette Goddard, who wears the diamond feather wraparound necklace by Flato.

A Flato ink and gouache drawing of Paulette Goddard's diamond feather wraparound necklace features a hidden clasp in the stem. The prototype for this design was the "Question Mark" necklace made by Boucheron in 1889.

Duchin, heartthrobs Douglas Fairbanks and Cesar Romero—right up to exalted cinematic talents Laurence Olivier and Orson Welles. What lured these luminaries to Flato was superb diamond jewelry and the lively atmosphere of his salon.

Jeanne Boivin did not make all-diamond jewels as often as Flato, preferring to work with semiprecious stones, but when she did use diamonds the results were always completely individual. From 1893 up to World War I, Jeanne Boivin's husband René headed the establishment, and almost every

A diamond and platinum Queen Anne's lace brooch has two stalks crowned with many tiny flower heads. Tucked away in the shadows, emerald and gold leaves twinkle. While most jewelers chose refined blooms for their subjects, such as the rose, Boivin went for the lacy clusters of the familiar tall roadside plant.

jewel made by the firm involved a nature theme. After his death in 1917, Jeanne Boivin carried on the business and, never embracing the fashion for Art Deco, continued to make nature-theme jewelry. Boivin's allegiance to nature and its fluid lines stemmed from her husband's jewelry designs as well as the loosely draped dresses, flower embroidery, and rose-inspired accessories of her younger brother, couturier Paul Poiret. In the mid-thirties, Boivin put her own distinctive imprint on diamond naturalism by choosing unusual plants and flowers—the foxglove, the catkin, and the humble Queen Anne's lace—to depict in diamonds. Her fluid organic style is beautifully expressed in the Queen Anne's lace brooch. She transformed the lacy white flower, one of her personal favorites, into a mass of small diamonds set in lozenge-shaped segments of platinum that appeared as brightly polished metal triangles flanking the diamonds, intensifying their sparkle. The balanced ratio of metal to gems revealed a daring originality, because most jewelers at this time were intent on concealing the mechanisms holding the gems in place.

By the late thirties and early forties, some jewelers were taking the nature theme beyond its antique origins. Two of these progressives, Suzanne Belperron and the Duke of Verdura, emerged from houses that had given new life to naturalism; Belperron had worked for Boivin and Verdura had worked for Chanel and Flato. As soon as they became independent, both designers soared creatively, reshuffling the deck and changing the rules of nature themes in fine jewelry.

In 1933 Belperron formed a partnership with Bernard Herz of B. Herz. It was at this firm that her name, jewelry, and fresh outlook became well known. Belperron went against the grain with her outspoken opinions on antique jewelry. She felt it was all right for "Aunt Agatha's neck in her day [but] worthless if it does nothing for the personality of the woman who has inherited it." Belperron believed women should wear contemporary jewelry, which she defined as organic, oversize, bulbous, and curvilinear, not as hard-edge architectural Art Deco. By her own emphatic decision, Belperron refused to sign her pieces. She claimed her jewelry was recognizable on sight, and it was truly unmistakable. When composing a jewel, Belperron laid stones on the floor to better assess their flash value from a distance at which they would normally be seen. The final products were large and unfailingly modern.

Although Belperron's favorite motifs, flowers and leaves, were common in jewelry, she transformed them with her unique point of view. She also manipulated the forms of pinecones, cattails, and grapes into designs that looked like no one else's. Pulling at the proportions of jewelry, she widened and heightened the dimensions by using chunky semiprecious stones: smoky topaz, crystal, and chalcedony. Diamonds added contrast, a tart sparkle to a dull shine. In one flower brooch, a thick piece of carved smoky topaz centers on a single diamond. The huge blossom emerges from a small platinum and diamond stem. Adventurous jewelry wearers, with the Duchess of Windsor at the top of the list, thrilled to Belperron's unconventional creations bulging with semiprecious stones and diamonds.

Verdura, who opened his own New York firm in 1939, was equally outspoken in his opinions about jewelry. He called large diamonds "mineralogy, not jewelry," and he dismissed solitaire diamonds in rings as "swimming pools." Still, as a titled Italian, Verdura was too much of a historian and old-world aesthete to completely deny diamonds their place in jewelry. He reduced their sway, however, in his own pieces. He chose gems such as zircons, yellow and brown sapphires, and precious pink topaz for the colors of flowers, fish, mermaids, shells, pomegranates, and leaves, the assortment of natural themes that characterized his work. Diamonds usually appeared as highlights. They added crisp light to the color schemes. When Verdura decorated his signature natural shell clips with diamonds, the gems resembled the foam of a wave breaking over the sunlit crustaceous surface.

As naturalism in jewelry moved further away from the antique—its original source of

A carved smoky topaz gives heft to a platinum and diamond flower brooch by Belperron, who was celebrated for her unique use of diamonds. A newspaper article reported, "Suzanne is unorthodox in her designing methods. She has been known, for instance, to sink a 15-carat marquise diamond into a scooped-out ring of rock crystal. Or to use hundreds of round and baguette diamonds to create glittering veins in crystal and thus produce clips and matching bracelets."

inspiration—it also moved away from all-diamond compositions. More color was added with precious as well as semiprecious gems. Themes changed according to fashion over the decades—from botanical to aerial to aquatic to fantasy. Nevertheless, it was the movement that began in the thirties with diamond jewelry that established naturalism as a perennial in twentieth-century precious jewelry.

Verdura chose a lion's paw shell for a clip brooch that belonged to Standard Oil heiress Millicent Rogers. Diamonds set in gold followed the shell's indentations. Collecting shells on the beaches of Fire Island and Florida and making them into precious jewelry was one of Verdura's favorite pursuits. His eye for nature and the thrill of the unexpected led him to the signature shell pieces that he created in various sizes and colors throughout his career. He was always changing the designs. When the lion's paw became extinct, he translated the shell into gold and enamel.

In a Horst photograph for *Vogue* (January 15, 1941) Paulette Goddard uses an orange lion's paw shell clip set with diamonds by Verdura to fasten her head scarf to a Hattie Carnegie cabana suit.

CHAPTER 6

GOLD AND DIAMONDS

"*G*old is news these days; news makes fashion, and fashion

is the life of business."

Jewelers' Circular (March 1934)

In April 1933 the United States abandoned the gold standard that had enabled anyone, in theory, to turn in dollars for gold. Jewelers had been taking in gold for its scrap value since platinum became the dominant metal for jewelry around 1900, and in increasing amounts since the 1929 stock-market crash. With the metal distanced from the financial sphere, large quantities became available at relatively inexpensive rates, and jewelers began returning it to the marketplace in huge, sculptural gold accessories studded with diamonds.

The shiny metal lent itself well to exaggerated machine-style jewelry, making for dramatic daytime accessories. From Paris to New York the look of gold and diamond jewelry was similar. A frank aesthetic touched everything from toasters to trains, and jewelry followed suit. Even though jewelers had been on the modernist track since Art Deco (with only a few defecting to diamond naturalism), gold and diamond jewelry took it to a new level. Gold jewelry went much further than Art Deco in its acceptance of modernity, penetrating beyond surface details of architecture to the guts of a building or a machine.

Industrial growth, with its factories and machines, helped to assuage the woes of the Depression and the dysfunctional economy. Assembly lines, labor-saving machines, and transportation—trains, cars, and planes—afforded jobs and mobility. Because these technologies were associated with a better future, every aspect of their design, as well as their function, was admired. Just as the skyscrapers of the Art Deco period put their imprint on jewelry design, the look of machines was the driving force behind gold jewelry.

The idolization of technology in the mid-thirties made industrial designers the art directors of change. They stripped their work of superfluous details and ornamentation and gloried in the aesthetic—and novel-looking—aspects of the working parts. Walter Dorwin Teague's Bantam Special for

A gold necklace made by Van Cleef & Arpels in 1943 features a double gas-pipe chain terminating in diamond-set knobs and a tassel with diamond-set balls. The details are deftly handled. Clustered diamonds of various sizes on the knobs provide balance and texture, and the transition from two to numerous gas-pipe chains is smooth, with a loop concealing the point of contact.

Kodak made in 1936 was a study in simplicity, every detail of the design connected to the camera's function. Even the horizontal bands across the case served to enclose the lacquer coating and protect the body from chipping. When Henry Dreyfuss designed the 300 Type Desk Set telephone for Bell in 1937 he worked from the inside out, reducing the machine to its essential components and packing them neatly in a smooth body and handset that was praised for its subtlety, efficiency, and modulated surfaces. The commitment to industry reached its zenith at the 1939 New York World's Fair. Its theme, "The World of Tomorrow," promised a better future with modern appliances and transportation easing the rigors of living.

Though gold jewelry had no function other than to adorn, it participated in the effort to make "Tomorrow" a visual reality by incorporating parts that looked as though they could operate in a machine. Unlike the flat, angular, gem-covered designs of Art Deco, gold jewelry was an assemblage of metal parts that came in the form of three-dimensional knobs, chains, balls, arcs, and domes. Sinuous, hollow, articulated cables called gas-pipe or snake chains were the most popular elements. They formed necklaces, bracelets, and watch bracelets. Flat gold rectangles linked together made straps described as brickwork. Protuberances called nail heads lined up in rows on bracelets appeared to have been fished out of a box of spare parts. A recessed step pattern was named an escalator design, bringing to mind a swift and easy passage between floors. The repetition of elements created the desired look of mechanical assemblage and even mass production.

Stacked disks form a multitiered pink gold ring with a diamond outline.

The gold employed in gold and diamond jewelry was generally 18 karat, an alloy composed of three-quarters gold, the remaining quarter made up of silver and copper. Pink gold, its color achieved by increasing the amount of copper, was a harder, stronger alloy applied in the main to clasps and attachments. But some jewelers exploited its aesthetic qualities and used it in highly sculptural gold and diamond jewelry.

Precious gems served as accents in the machinelike gold jewels, with the emphasis of the design on the metal parts. The reduced number of gems also kept down the price. Emeralds, rubies, sapphires, and diamonds were all applied in almost equal measure, but diamonds proved superior to the others in gold jewelry. The metal surfaces often overwhelmed the colors of the other precious stones, whereas the sparkle of diamonds held its own on the expansive gold spaces.

Many jewelers maintained the steady traffic flow in their salons during the thirties by creating imaginative gold jewelry. Trabert & Hoeffer, Inc.-Mauboussin, an American firm with offices in New York and Los Angeles and Paul Flato's biggest competitor for the movie star clientele, introduced its gold line with the name "Reflection—Your Personality in a Jewel." The "Reflection" jewels took advantage of casting technology that allowed the firm to fabricate jewels with standardized elements. A client could put them together any way she liked to create a jewel that fit her personality. She could also decide the placement of precious gems to further customize the look. While the pieces in this line of jewelry were not entirely handmade, they

Princess Hohenlohe, wife of a Polish diplomat posted in Washington, D.C., wears gold and diamond machine-style jewelry in a Horst photograph for *Vogue* (September 15, 1940). The crisp gold edges give the jewels a mechanical look.

were hand-finished and cost-effective. Design-it-yourself assemblage was a clever idea that made it possible to commission a one-of-a-kind piece—a privilege that had previously been the prerogative of a select few.

As a rule, gold was considered casual and sporty, appropriate only for daytime wear. Because platinum enhanced the whiteness and sparkle of diamonds, it had long been favored for formal evening jewelry. After the outbreak of World War II, though, that fashion edict changed. Women gravitated to large gold jewels in much the same way they did to flamboyant hats. Both accessories defied wartime austerity. The whimsical and highly feminine hats prompted a smile and conveyed an optimistic spirit and the bulky jewels refused to recede into the background.

The switch to gold, however, signaled more than merely a whim of style. Almost all of the platinum, a vital strategic metal used by the military as a catalyst for fuel and explosives, had been siphoned off into the war effort. In France the demand for platinum and wartime shortages led to new regulations for precious metals in jewelry. Clients were required to provide 135 percent of the metal necessary for a platinum jewel and 100 percent of the metal for a gold jewel. The manufacture of gold jewels with mechanical parts kept some jewelers afloat during the Nazi occupation of Paris. The accomplished French jewelers and manufacturers directed their superb skills to the gold style, resulting in some remarkable and forward-looking examples of craftsmanship and design.

During the war years, Joseph Chaumet's son Marcel ran the firm in Paris with a skeletal staff and managed to produce some of the most brazen gold jewelry of the period. Frédéric Boucheron's son Louis, who ran the family firm during the war, espoused the gold and diamond style, which he felt provided an opportunity for design innovation in heavy gold pieces. Van Cleef & Arpels, another French jeweler, took up the gold and diamond style and turned it into a lyrical statement with cascading gas pipes in necklaces elegantly studded with diamonds. The firm had participated in the 1939 New York World's Fair and at the close of the fair, it opened a branch at 744 Fifth Avenue. The success of the American venture tided Van Cleef & Arpels over during the war and positioned it to become one of the top two jewelers of the postwar period.

In America women stopped wearing platinum jewelry almost entirely, bought virtually no new pieces, and sold or donated old ones to aid the cause. One of the best-known jewelry lovers to do so was Mae West, who gave up her platinum and diamond collection to benefit the Royal Air Force. For the duration of the war, gold replaced platinum as the most popular metal for jewelry.

Its minimal diamond requirements meant the gold style remained unaffected by the World War II diamond shortage, which made the manu-

A gargantuan gold bracelet by Chaumet features repetitive ball and arc motifs; small diamonds accent the petal designs spread over the gold balls.

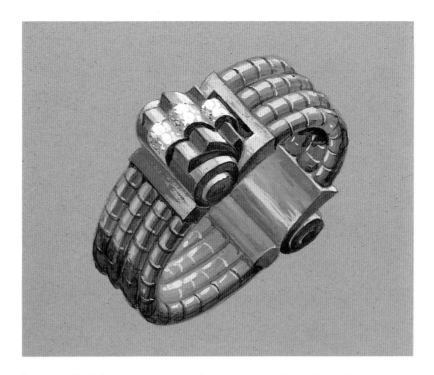

An ink and gouache drawing by Verger from around 1937 shows a quadruple cable bracelet with knob and step motifs accented by diamonds.

facture of all-diamond jewelry almost impossible. When the Germans invaded the diamond-cutting centers of the Low Countries, the price of diamonds jumped 50 percent. The production of polished melée, the single-cut diamonds (ranging from 0.05 to 0.20 carats) used in pavé settings, came to a standstill once the factories of Holland and Belgium shut down. Diamond cutters fled to New York, taking their tools with them. When possible, they hid their larger tools and machinery to prevent them from falling into enemy hands. In New York they found that only stones of high quality and larger size could be cut profitably, and a number of them moved on to Puerto Rico and Cuba to set up shops for melée production. Even with the influx of European lapidaries, the overall supply of diamonds plunged.

After the war, women returned to platinum as their first choice for the setting of diamonds. Gold jewelry remained popular but retreated back to daytime status and decreased in size when the enthusiasm for the machine aesthetic waned. Nevertheless, the vestigial remains of the style persisted in gold jewelry. The manufacture of standardized small parts had improved with wartime production and breakthroughs in casting techniques. François Verger, the grandson of the founder of Verger, returned to Paris after the war, prepared to reenter the jewelry industry. He had been wounded while serving with the United States forces in Asia, and after recovering in a United States veterans hospital, he boarded a plane with a casting machine under his arm. Henceforth his firm would be identified with fine gold bracelets incorporating repetitive motifs. The repeat motif popularized by machine mania became the mainstay of gold jewelry. And for these jewels, diamonds continued to be the most successful and stylish gem accent.

DIAMONDS ARE A GIRL'S BEST FRIEND

Formal diamond jewelry enjoyed a grand comeback after World War II. The regalia worn by British nobility at Elizabeth II's wedding in 1947 and her coronation in 1953 was a powerful factor in the revival. These events made pieces with royal provenance and impressive diamond suites—with necklaces, bracelets, earrings, and even tiaras—a regular part of the etiquette of formal dressing. Leading jewelers Harry Winston and Van Cleef & Arpels allied themselves with the passion for royalty and opulent accessories, and by doing so they eclipsed every other precious jeweler of the era. With museum-quality collections, both used antique diamond jewelry as an integral part of their image. At the same time, they created modern diamond jewelry with huge clusters of marquise and pear shapes and rows of baguettes that was lavish enough for any court occasion. A beacon of the postwar prosperity, the well-dressed woman wore lots of diamond accessories, making the period one of the most diamond-oriented. The love of diamonds even extended to popular culture. In the movie *Gentlemen Prefer Blondes* (1953), when Marilyn Monroe sang "Diamonds Are a Girl's Best Friend," she summed up the jubilant attitude toward the gem and gave it a new tag.

Jewelers had introduced a regal, all-diamond style for every British coronation since Edward VII's in 1902. Delicate platinum and diamond jewelry based on the Versailles code of motifs was the favored mode when Edward VII took the throne and continued in popularity through George V's 1911 investiture. In 1937, when George VI became king, diamond naturalism, inspired by the platinum and diamond style of the previous two coronations, came into vogue. After Elizabeth II's 1953 coronation, the platinum and diamond styles from the early part of the century lent inspiration to Harry Winston and Van Cleef & Arpels as well. However, the two jewelers did not linger on the representational motifs of the Versailles code. What impressed them was the size and impact of the British crown jewelry. The contemporary work of Harry Winston and Van Cleef & Arpels featured good-size, fancy-cut diamonds with the platinum mountings hidden so as not to distract from the stones. To heighten the flash value, jewels were often made and worn in matching suites. Some of the necklaces had large diamonds worthy of a queen. These jewelers almost never employed melée; the small diamonds found in pavé settings had no place in most of their designs.

When Marilyn Monroe belted out "Diamonds Are a Girl's Best Friend" in *Gentlemen Prefer Blondes* (1953), a new piece of lore was added to the age-old gem.

The promotion of diamond jewelry by such firms as Winston and Van Cleef & Arpels received reinforcement from De Beers, the company that controlled most of the world's diamond production and trade. Diamond markets had taken a beating during World War II. In order to revive the gem's standing, De Beers entered the arena as a major player in the promotion of diamonds. While the royal family was touring South Africa in April 1947, De Beers turned the occasion of Princess Elizabeth of England's twenty-first birthday into a diamond fete. The first item on the agenda that day was a visit to the Big Hole at Kimberley. Once the mighty source of diamonds, the depleted mine had been turned into a tourist attraction. After the excursion De Beers hosted a birthday luncheon at an exclusive haunt of diamond magnates, the Kimberley Club. In the course of the celebrations Elizabeth received a diamond jewel from the De Beers collection. Other birthday presents came in the form of diamonds. Schoolchildren from Southern Rhodesia presented her with an all-diamond brooch in the shape of the flame lily of their land, and the South African government gave her a necklace with twenty-one brilliant-cut diamonds.

The importance of the royal family to diamonds cannot be overestimated, since the royals' popularity climbed to an all-time high after the war. The king and queen had stayed in London during the blitz, setting an example of English courage. With their two daughters, they represented the ideal of morals and behavior. A *Vogue* (November 1, 1949) article on the British monarchy described the stature of three generations of royal women: "Queen Mary is perhaps the most distinguished public woman living in the world today. Her daughter-in-law, the present Queen of England, and her granddaughter, the Princess Elizabeth, are the center, in their own right, of every stage they occupy."

Princess Elizabeth took center stage with diamonds blazing when she married the Duke of Edinburgh in 1947. Enchanting as a fairy tale, her wedding had the side effect of making formality fashionable and appropriate. The images of Elizabeth and the nobility wearing diamond jewels made a deep impression, and De Beers followed up on the enthusiasm, prevailing on the royals to loan the two jewels Elizabeth had been given in South Africa as well as two wedding gifts for its exhibit at the British Industries Fair in London. Queen Mary's present to the bride, an eighteen-inch-long, turn-of-the-century diamond stomacher, lay alongside her parents' gift of pendant earrings with fancy-cut diamonds at the De Beers display. To publicize the event, De Beers took out full-page advertisements in magazines on both sides of the Atlantic, making pictures of the jewels familiar in detail to the public.

The magnificent necklaces and earrings presented in the De Beers exhibit and worn by the nobility at the wedding dazzled the public. Tiaras had such an impact that they made a comeback. This many commoners had not worn tiaras since the turn of the century. Women purchased antique tiaras or commissioned modern headgear for formal parties, balls, and opening nights, if not for the second dazzling occasion in London, the coronation of Elizabeth II in 1953.

At Buckingham Palace, Elizabeth poses in a suite of diamond jewelry for a photograph taken in 1953, the year of the coronation. She wears the King George IV state diadem with a wedding present from the leading businessmen of London, a nineteenth-century Russian-style diamond fringe necklace. Her fancy-cut diamond pendant earrings were a wedding gift from her parents. The brooch on her shoulder was the smallest section of Queen Mary's stomacher, another present to the royal bride. The quick succession of the wedding and crowning kept regal diamond jewelry highly visible. At the time of the wedding to Prince Philip in 1947, a display of 2,660 gifts in St. James Palace was open to the public, with the proceeds of the admission price going to charity. For the coronation even more of Elizabeth's diamond wedding gifts as well as crown jewels were in evidence.

The transfer of the British throne was obviously no small affair. The ritual went back almost nine hundred years, to William the Conqueror. At the coronation and surrounding festivities Elizabeth displayed some of the items that the public had seen at the De Beers exhibit. She wore the bottom half of Queen Mary's stomacher as a brooch and the modern diamond earrings from her parents. Each jewel Elizabeth wore, and every other aspect of the ceremony and guest list, was detailed in newspapers and magazines. *Vogue* alone dedicated fourteen pages to the major players in the pageant. Photographs by Cecil Beaton and Norman Parkinson featured such attendants as the ladies of the bedchamber, the mistress of the robes, the train bearers, and the maids of honor, all of them wearing diamond jewelry, contemporary as well as inherited pieces from their noble families.

The De Beers campaign was not restricted to the British crown jewels. The firm supported diamond jewelry at every level. Since it could not open an office in America (one of the most important markets for diamonds) because of antitrust laws, N. W. Ayer ran the advertising campaign and promotions. Ayer processed information and prepared press releases for the media on all aspects of diamonds, from diamond cutting to diamond jewelry fashions. The advertising firm arranged for movie stars to wear diamonds in

The fashionable Duchess of Kent in court dress wears an array of inherited diamond jewelry from her royal family. Pictures like this one, published in American *Vogue* (April 15, 1953), helped make antique jewelry and tiaras popular among commoners.

their screen roles and spread the word on diamonds in seminars for women's groups and high school assemblies, making sure no potential customer was overlooked.

Beyond the day-to-day push, a single line from N. W. Ayer has done more for the diamond's allure than any other promotion. The ad line came to Frances Gerety one night when she was completing her assignment for the 1948 presentation to De Beers. As Gerety remembers it, "Dog tired, I put my head down and said, 'Please God, send me a line.'" Then she wrote, "A diamond is forever." The next morning Gerety knew she had "something good." And indeed she did. The phrase has gone beyond copywriters' classics and entered the vernacular.

The "forever" phrase conjured up the history and durability of diamonds as well as their romance. It was splashed across the sophisticated De Beers "Great Artist" series of diamond ads in which commissioned work from contemporary painters Pablo Picasso, André Derain, Salvador Dalí, Marie Laurencin, and Raoul Dufy linked diamonds with fine art. Practical information for judging the quality of diamonds was expressed in plain type as "The 4C's." The heading encapsulated the four variables—clarity, color, cut, and carat weight—to be considered when purchasing a diamond engagement ring.

The flood of GI's coming home after the war led to a marriage boom and a great need for information about diamond engagement rings—a design centering on a solitaire diamond, a single gem usually uplifted by prongs and exposed to the light. For this design it is important to have a quality stone. In diamond jewels with a number of stones, each and every gem is not as closely scrutinized; a little flaw in a pavé setting, for example, cannot be detected by the naked eye, nor does it take away from the entire effect.

In choosing the diamond for an engagement ring, carat weight, or size, is a personal preference. Cut refers to the arrangement of facets and the reflection of light. A good cut has the most brilliance. In regard to color, the finest white diamonds are colorless or near colorless; tints of yellow or brown in a stone reduce its attractiveness and value. Clarity refers to the number of inclusions (internal characteristics such as a fracture, a chip or break, or a knot, an included diamond crystal) in a gem. The best diamonds are called flawless, meaning no irregularity is visible under ten-power magnification. These educational tools, couched in sumptuous artistic advertisements, did their part in turning the postwar period into an era when people not only wore diamonds but were knowledgeable about what they were wearing. In its far-reaching strategy, De Beers understood the relationship between crown jewel exhibits and engagement ring education. Brides with knowledge about their diamonds had a proprietary interest in Elizabeth II's diamond jewelry presents, and the exhibit of royal gifts could whet their appetites to purchase more diamond jewelry.

Almost as influential as the royal family in diamond matters and right up there with De Beers, Harry Winston burst into the news in the early 1950s with his blockbuster collection of big diamonds. A *Life* (March 17, 1952) magazine article entitled "Golconda on E. 51st" explained, "Insofar as connoisseurs in these matters are aware, the British royal family owns the world's biggest collection of historic jewels. The second biggest, however, is owned by a U. S. citizen, not widely known to the general public, whose name is Harry Winston. While the royal family collection, including as it does the two largest cut diamonds in the world, Cullinan I and Cullinan II, as well as the Kohinoor and the Black Prince ruby, is an enviable one, it is only fair to point out that in acquiring it the Windsor family and their predecessors have had certain competitive advantages. For one thing they have been collecting fine stones for more than 500 years and have been presented with many world-famous gems. For another, the loyal subjects who have made the presentations have been able, for the past few decades, to count on the resources and cooperation of the British-owned De Beers diamond monopoly which controls 95% of the world diamond production. In contrast Winston has been collecting gems for a mere 33 years and entirely on his own."

Winston's $10 million collection, dubbed the Court of Jewels, included some of the best-known diamonds in the world. The 44.5-carat Hope—made famous by its curse, blue color, and royal French provenance—and the 100-carat Star of the East from the Evalyn Walsh McLean estate formed the centerpieces. The third headliner, the 126-carat Jonker, came from a 726-carat rough stone. A 60-carat emerald-cut diamond ring originated in the collection of Mabel Boll, America's "Queen of Diamonds." In the "world's largest" department there were the Indore Pears of 44.63 and 44.18 carats, the largest perfectly matched twin diamonds in the world, and the 72-carat Idol's Eye, the largest blue diamond in the world. The 31.26-carat McLean diamond, also from Evalyn Walsh's estate, rounded out the exhibit. (Two gem-set jewels, the Dudley necklace and the Inquisition necklace, and a few colored stones played a subsidiary role to the big diamonds in the grouping.)

The son of a jeweler, Winston began his career watching and assisting his father in his small Los Angeles jewelry store. In 1920, at the age of twenty-four, he started his own firm, Premier Diamond Company, at 537 Fifth Avenue in New York. He purchased estates with nineteenth-century and turn-of-the-century pieces that people were selling in order to buy Art Deco jewelry. They considered antique styles outmoded and the diamond shapes worthless in comparison with the new brilliant and modern geometric-shaped diamonds like the baguette. Winston made his money by recutting the diamonds to heighten their brilliance, reselling them loose or setting them in contemporary jewelry. Over the years he kept upgrading the quality of every aspect of his business. In 1932, he incorporated his company under his own name.

Harry Winston's Court of Jewels toured the United States, Europe, and Cuba for ten years. The exhibit was almost always booked for benefits and civic functions. In New York, the price of admission raised money for the United Hospital Fund. Ilka Chase, chairman of the UHF Arts Projects Committee, wrote a catalogue giving a brief history of each gem and jewel on display. At the opening party at Rockefeller Center, Eleanor Steber from the Metropolitan Opera sang the "Jewel Song" from Faust, and Francis Henry

Taylor, director of the Metropolitan Museum of Art, acted as master of ceremonies. In San Antonio, Texas, members of the Junior League modeled Winston's Court of Jewels at the Symphony Jewel Ball to benefit the Symphony Society.

Mrs. John McFarlin, a member of the San Antonio Junior League, models the Hope diamond at a 1952 charity ball to raise money for the Symphony Society. The Hope diamond was part of Harry Winston's Court of Jewels, a collection he offered to charities and nonprofit organizations as the focal point for fund-raising events. The popularity of the "Court" helped educate the public and create an enthusiasm for diamonds.

Some of the pieces in the collection were sold to people as famous as the gems themselves. The Duchess of Windsor picked up the McLean diamond and King Farouk took the Jonker and the Star of the East. When pieces left the exhibit, new ones of equal caliber took their place. At the 1954 Texas State Fair in Dallas, the flawless blue-white 62.05-carat Winston diamond made its public debut. Though the stone had just been cut from a 154.5-carat rough, the history of the gem was familiar to readers of *The New Yorker* (May 8 and 15, 1954). A lengthy two-part profile by Lillian Ross called "The Big Stone" documented its voyage from a piece of South African rough purchased from a London dealer through its cutting by Winston's lapidary. Along the way, Winston "was gradually reaching the conclusion that he had come into possession of a truly remarkable stone; in his more buoyant moments he was beginning to feel that in its color and purity it was equal, if not superior, to the celebrated Jonker diamond that nearly twenty years before he had split up into twelve smaller diamonds, the largest of which he sold for a million dollars. Winston's enthusiasm for his new diamond had

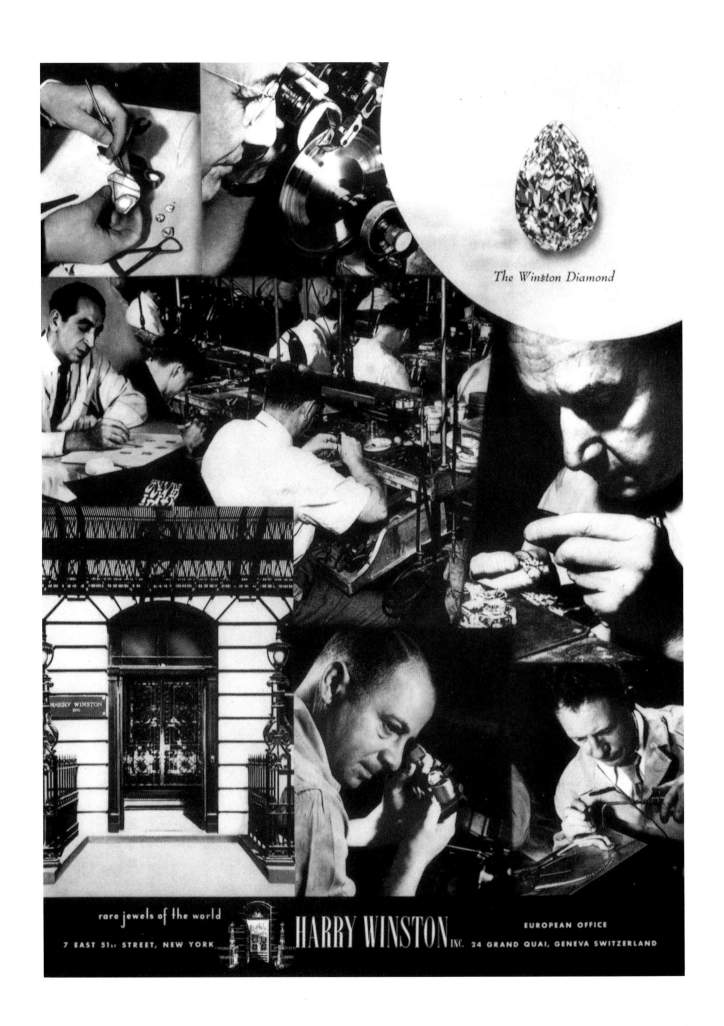

The Winston Diamond

rare jewels of the world

HARRY WINSTON INC.

7 EAST 51st STREET, NEW YORK

EUROPEAN OFFICE
24 GRAND QUAI, GENEVA SWITZERLAND

A pictorial essay in a Winston ad illustrates the cutting of the 62.05-carat Winston diamond. Winston's cutter begins the process by using India ink to mark the cleavage plane for the 154.5-carat rough and then the blocker cuts sixteen facets to give the stone its pear shape. Designs worked out on paper are part of the problem-solving process, one that invariably revolves around the trade-off between carat weight and brilliance (removing impurities to add to the brilliance results in weight loss). The next stage is handled by a brillianteer, who breaks down the main facets into smaller ones and refines the shape of the stone. After many months spent cutting the diamond, the gem is mounted in a jewel.

been only lukewarm at first—for one thing, he had been disappointed to find that a piece was missing, having apparently cracked off in the remote geological past—but as time went on and his chief cutter removed the stone's skin, or outer coating, creating 'windows' that revealed a flawless interior and a striking blue-white color, he had come to have a deep attachment for it." Winston's diamond was featured with some of the stars of the Court of Jewels such as the Hope, along with a 90-carat briolette diamond (a teardrop shape with triangular facets on all sides) and the 127.02-carat Portuguese diamond. The latter gem supposedly came from the Portuguese crown jewels, but this has never been authenticated. However, the gem did have at least one colorful owner before Harry Winston. It was the pride and joy of Ziegfeld Follies girl Peggy Hopkins-Joyce, who flaunted it in her publicity stills and a fashion portrait by photographer Edward Steichen (see page 66).

One of Winston's motivations for assembling the Court of Jewels collection was to educate the public about what good diamonds should look like in color, clarity, and cut. There was no greater champion of jewelry and gem education than Winston. He ran a "diamond school" in his New York establishment in addition to his jewelry workshop and lapidary. At the school, students learned how to grade and judge the quality of diamonds. Occasionally Winston would bring them to the salon to experience the thrill of selling expensive diamond jewelry, and after the course they either worked for Winston or disseminated their skills throughout the jewelry industry. Another aspect of Winston's crusade was to inspire Americans to wear gems worthy of their wealth or position of power in the world. In fact, one of Winston's pet goals was to establish a national gem collection. It was an idea laid out in a 1960 syndicated article by Ilka Chase, a tongue-in-cheek piece for a country of diamond lovers without a collection of crown jewels: "The Winston dream for American womanhood is to see established a state collection of superb jewels which would belong to the nation as the crown jewels of Great Britain belong to the English and which would be worn on ceremonious or festive occasions by the wives of our presidents, cabinet officers, and possibly . . . if there was enough to go around . . . by the wives of the members of the Supreme Court. Mr. Winston feels that such treasure would be heartwarming on domestic occasions and that it is downright indispensable for international barbecues."

Chase went on to fantasize about the possibilities of such a national jewelry box. "One can see his reasoning. Suppose the day comes . . . and well it might . . . when there is a woman president and she entertains or is entertained by a Queen of England or (and who shall say it can't happen?) the female head of the Union of Socialist Soviet Republicans who, fed to the teeth with the dictatorship of the proletariat, is blazing like a five alarm fire with the crown jewels of all the Russians? Is our girl supposed to stand mousy and wren-like beside them? Not while the patriotic heart of Harry Winston beats beneath his conservatively tailored business suit."

Though Winston's dream did not come true exactly the way he envisioned it, he did carry through on his part. Beginning in 1958, Winston gave several of his best and most valuable gems and jewels to the American public, as he imagined others would have done if there had been a national gem collection established in Washington, D.C. The Winston donation to the Smithsonian Institution included the Hope diamond, the Portuguese diamond, and the Inquisition necklace. These gifts, on permanent display, have boosted the popularity of gems and minerals. The Hope diamond alone has become the most popular item in the entire museum complex.

Winston's achievement in putting together the Court of Jewels with such outstanding specimens made his name synonymous with diamonds internationally. Nobility from around the world, and those who wanted to look like nobility, headed to Winston. Winston concocted many styles of simple diamond necklaces to display the huge diamond showpieces. The most popular was his V-shaped line of round, marquise, and pear-shaped diamonds in different combinations. Though their shapes did not detract from the large stones and appeared deceptively simple in necklace designs, the marquise and pear shapes were the most expensive diamond shapes, because they were the most difficult to cut. When fancy-cut diamonds were at their peak of popularity in Art Deco jewelry, the marquise appeared only sporadically and the pear shape almost never turned up. Harry Winston—and Van Cleef & Arpels—designed almost all their diamond jewelry around fancy-cut diamonds, with the marquise and pear shape leading the way.

Winston's jewelry with holly wreath settings played up these two cuts even more than the fancy-cut large-diamond pendant necklaces. The style grew out of his dissatisfaction with typical platinum settings, which he felt swamped the diamonds in metal and flattened them out. The idea for the setting came as a Christmas gift one year when Winston looked at the holly wreath on the door of his house. He recognized it as the perfect analogy for the jewelry he wanted to make. The shape of the leaves inspired his layout of marquise and pear-shaped diamonds, and the hidden attachments of the wreath prompted a flexible arrangement of platinum wires that lifted the diamonds into the light and let them shine. Winston's holly wreath setting for necklaces and earrings made the diamonds in the finished jewels look like clusters of gems held together magically.

Winston carried over the same principle of many gems and little metal into his bracelets. One of the styles featured all different shapes of gems, massed higgledy-piggledy, in sharp contrast to the flat, wide Art Deco bracelets that met with Winston's disapproval. His bracelets were so flexible they could be crumpled like a sweater, yet so well manufactured that the diamonds never banged into each other, which could scratch the facets.

Van Cleef & Arpels, Winston's biggest rival, also specialized in diamond jewelry and had museum-quality goods in its small collection of historic pieces, including a group of three jewels dubbed Napoleon's Court. The tiara Napoleon I supposedly placed on Josephine's head at their coronation ceremony was the centerpiece. Composed of 880 diamonds weighing about 260 carats, the jewel had an overall butterfly design that curved to a widow's peak in the front, an unusual feature for tiaras of this period. The two other

The holly wreath motif of the Winston necklace is carried over into the bracelet. This extraordinarily rich suite of diamond jewelry is characteristic of the postwar period, when women enjoyed a unified look in their contemporary diamond pieces.

jewels were Napoleon's wedding gifts to his second wife, Marie-Louise, a diamond and emerald tiara by Nitot and a matching necklace.

The jewels in Napoleon's Court were not always shown as a group; sometimes they went their separate ways. Josephine's tiara, for example, became a familiar window decoration at Van Cleef & Arpels. Marie-Louise's tiara, on the other hand, was a party goer. Van Cleef & Arpels loaned it to Marjorie Merriweather Post to wear at a Red Cross function in Palm Beach. The beauty of the emeralds, however, proved irresistible to the jeweler, who broke Marie-Louise's tiara down and remounted all 135 emeralds into contemporary pieces. The act sparked broad media coverage. One glossy maga-

A Winston diamond bracelet features a multitude of round and pear-shaped diamonds in a couple of sizes. The customary rectangular frame mounting was abandoned in Winston bracelets for minimal mountings that allow the shapes of the gems to define the contours.

The 1957 cover of the Van Cleef & Arpels New York catalogue left no doubt about the origin of the firm's diamond jewelry.

zine published before and after shots in color with images of the intact tiara and the array of new jewels made from its gems. Marjorie Merriweather Post bought the diamond shell of the tiara and filled the mount with turquoise. (In the mid-sixties, Post donated the tiara to the Smithsonian, as well as two items she had purchased from Harry Winston: an all-diamond necklace Napoleon gave to Marie-Louise at the birth of the king of Rome and the 31-carat Blue Heart diamond, also referred to as the Eugénie Blue, because it was once believed to be part of the empress's collection.)

The international firm of Van Cleef & Arpels was run by the Arpels family. (Charles Van Cleef had died some years earlier.) Although they had stores in many American cities, the Arpels stressed their French origins. In the firm's American advertisements, it juxtaposed modern diamond jewels with views of the Place Vendôme and French ocean liners. A French bias came across clearly in all its formal diamond suites of necklaces and earrings. Van Cleef & Arpels proudly implemented the old Versailles code of motifs, flowers, bows, and ribbons, but to very different effect than its predecessors. Good-size diamonds blazed, with metal kept to a minimum. The flowers were transformed into bolder designs with large marquise and pear-shaped diamonds, and the scrolling bows and ribbons were rendered in baguettes.

Creative designs with charming names characterized the smaller diamond pieces that repeatedly drew clients to Van Cleef & Arpels to supplement their formal suites. Diamond earrings called "Cheek Kissers" brushed the cheeks instead of simply covering the lobes. "Cascade" and "Rain" aptly described the brooches with streams of diamonds tumbling over volutes and semicircles. The "Wheat Sheaf" brooch had two crossed stalks with rectangular and brilliant-cut diamond grains; both featured baguette-cut diamond stems. They were frequently clipped in the hair like barrettes, offering a less elaborate alternative to the tiara. The style was given a boost when First Lady Jackie Kennedy wore a few Van Cleef & Arpels brooches, the "Wheat Sheaf" and the "Flame" (a pavé-set string bean-shaped design from the thirties), in her hair during the 1961 state visit to Paris. The gem fireworks prompted the press to give copy to her jewels and background history on how she wore them. Under a head shot in the *New York Herald Tribune,* the caption read, "Another Day Another Hairdo" and "Flame shaped diamond clips held her tresses in the Louis XIV Court style

Opposite: During a 1961 state visit to Paris, President John F. Kennedy escorts the First Lady, Jackie, to a gala at Versailles hosted by President and Mme Charles de Gaulle. To accessorize her Givenchy evening dress, Jackie wore several Van Cleef & Arpels brooches, "Wheat Sheaf" and "Flame," in her hair. For the September 21, 1963, column "D.C. Wash," Gerry Van Der Heuvel summed up the effect of her diamonds: "During the Kennedy's state visit to Paris in May, 1961, she set European society on its ear when she appeared with tiny diamond clips forming a small circlet around her hair—not a tiara, mind you, merely the suggestion of one. And here in the U.S. Americans burst their buttons with pride."

The 1956 "Wheat Sheaf" diamond brooch by Van Cleef & Arpels with baguettes and circular cuts is the same design as the pair worn by Jackie Kennedy in Paris.

fashionable in the seventeenth century when Versailles social life was at its peak." *Life* magazine illustrated a picture of the First Lady beside a portrait of the duchesse de Fontanges, Louis XIV's mistress, who was the inspiration for Jackie's hairstyle, dubbed "Fontanges 1961."

When talking about their jewelry to the press, the Arpels frequently explained how difficult it was to assemble the diamonds and the challenges of cutting and matching them. A press release for June 1953 stated, "Van Cleef & Arpels has pieces in which the 300 or more diamonds are not only matched for color and size, but are all cut by the same diamond-cutter! Although he is an exact workman who must adhere to the established form of grinding-on the facets, every diamond cutter has his own personality, and when a mass of stones is to be set pavé and must look like one surface, 'all-over setting,' it makes for uniformity to have one man cut all the gems."

The attention to the details of diamonds and diamond cutting stemmed from the firm's history. In the mid-nineteenth century, Charles Van Cleef was a diamond cutter in Amsterdam who distinguished himself through his wizardry in recutting flawed diamonds no one else would touch. He later emigrated to Paris to take advantage of the opportunities for a jeweler in that city, where he also found success. In fact, Van Cleef was one of

the lucky few who walked away from the auction of the Diamonds of the Crown of France a happy man, having obtained a diamond floweret from Empress Eugénie's collection. It may be a coincidence, but ever after the firm put flowers first in its list of favorite motifs. In 1898, Van Cleef's son Alfred joined forces with his wife's brothers Charles and Julien Arpels, who came from a family of diamond dealers. At Van Cleef & Arpels the passion for diamonds has passed on from generation to generation.

Coming from different directions, America and France, but linked by their appreciation for museum-quality jewels and beautiful diamonds, Winston and Van Cleef & Arpels shared many clients who happily shopped at both establishments. Ann Warner, wife of the movie mogul Jack Warner, bought holly wreath diamond earrings at Winston and an earring and necklace suite at Van Cleef & Arpels. Marjorie Merriweather Post built her antique collection with purchases from both the Court of Jewels and Napoleon's Court. In an ever-widening circle of diamond mania, other jewelers profited from the popularity of the all-white style, turning out diamond jewelry in innumerable variations on the forms made famous by these two firms.

A vignette from *The New Yorker* profile of Winston illustrates the diamond's ubiquitous presence. He asked his secretary to list the ads featuring Winston jewels as accessories that week, and her reply gave the high and low of American consumerism: Cadillac, Parliament, Tabu, Maximilian Furs, Lucky Strike, and Revlon Nail Enamel. Entrepreneurial showmanship, like ads and publicity campaigns, dovetailed with decidedly nonmercantile events, like the royal wedding and coronation, which sustained the public's fascination with the gem. The diamond had made the crossover from a luxury hidden behind the closed doors of formal occasions or locked up in vaults to a topic of general interest.

Ann Warner's Van Cleef & Arpels necklace has an interior row of baguettes, a detail typical of diamond necklaces of the period, and an exterior row of marquise-cut diamonds. The strands of gems form a tassel with three pear-shaped diamonds of 16.18, 12.73, and 9.81 carats.

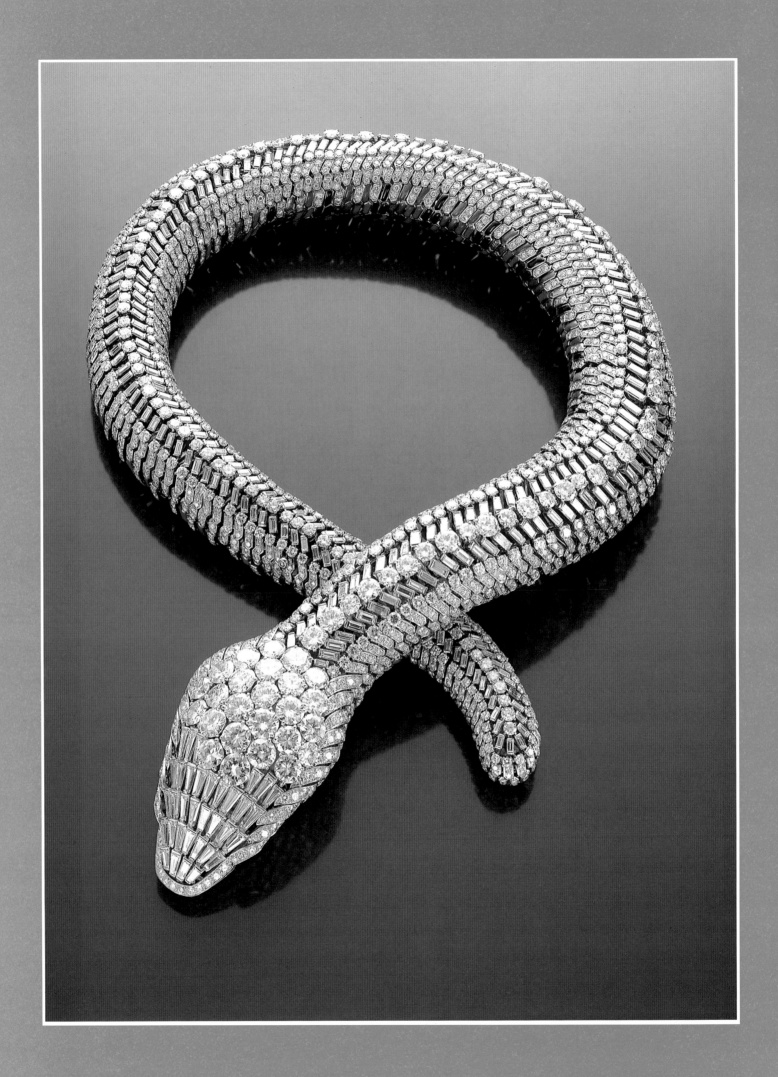

CHAPTER 8

THE CREATIVE JEWELERS

Mexican film actress Maria Felix
commissioned the snake necklace
from Cartier-Paris in 1968. The jewel
features 2,473 diamonds in
circular, baguette, and tapered
baguette cuts mounted in platinum.
Two emerald eyes (hidden in the
photograph) peer out from the sides
of the head. Conceived by Cartier
designer Gabriel Raton, the jewel
met with the approval of Jeanne
Toussaint, who helped refine the
many complex elements, such as the
arrangement of diamond scales, the
red, black, and green enamel scales,
and the clever circular-cut diamond
peg clasp that holds the necklace
together in one big coil at its
crossover point. A unique feature of
the jewel is its reversibility: the snake
could be worn with the diamonds on
the outside or turned around with
the enamel side outermost.

At midcentury, when Harry Winston and Van Cleef & Arpels were capturing the public's attention with museum-quality collections of diamonds and historic jewels, another group of jewelers was also forging links with the art world, but in a very different way. Jean Schlumberger, Pierre Sterlé, Julius Cohen, Seaman Schepps, David Webb, and Jeanne Toussaint thought of jewelry as an art form, and they approached its design as such. They traveled, haunted museums, and built up libraries of illustrated books for inspiration. Depicting representational subjects culled from nature, art, and the fantasy world, these jewelers painted with enamel and gems and sculpted in metal. Gold, a conspicuous element in many designs, provided form and texture. It was worked into spiky, granulated, and fringed decorations. In addition to gold, many jewels featured platinum as a plain mounting for diamonds. Enamel, unlike its delicate application at the turn of the century, was slathered on, coloring a frog's skin or delineating a snake's scales. Semiprecious gems, in opaque varieties like turquoise and transparent ones like morganite, served as center stones and accents. Sapphires, emeralds, and rubies took over some designs, but more often they were reduced to small, colorful details, like a zebra's ruby eyes or a sea serpent's emerald jaws. Frequently diamonds spread across the entire surface of jewels. They were also concentrated in a few key areas, contrasting with enamel or semiprecious stones. The addition of canary diamonds brought an intense complementary twin-tone sparkle to diamond jewelry.

Up to this time canary diamonds had appeared only sporadically in jewelry. Because Americans, especially Tiffany, had used them the most, Europeans considered canaries a fanciful American taste. In the mid-fifties, an infusion of canary diamonds from mines in South Africa brought about a reevaluation of the gem, led by the creative jewelers, who recognized the beauty of the lemon yellow–colored diamonds that fell into a completely different color classification from the white ones. When these gems appeared, the Gemological Institute of America (GIA), an educational and research center of the industry that provides Diamond Quality Grading Reports, had to revamp its system. Whereas the grading system in use had been based on the absence of yellow in diamonds—it went from D, the best "colorless" stones, to Z, stones with an unattractive yellowish cast (brought about by an admixture of the non-metallic chemical nitrogen)—it expanded to accommodate the presence of pure yellow in the canary diamonds. These gems were given the label "fancy."

Creative jewelers mounted them in gold, a metal that enhanced their color.

Personal style, expressed with canary diamonds and a host of other materials, was the criterion by which creative jewelers were judged and elevated to the level of artists. Many were following in the footsteps of such mid-thirties mavericks as Belperron and Verdura, who shocked with their high and low combinations. Having strength in numbers, the creative jewelers broke the cycle of uniform styles, such as Art Deco and fifties formalism, by establishing the importance of individuality.

In order to stimulate creativity with diamonds during the postwar years, De Beers staged diamond jewelry fashion shows annually. Given the deluge of applicants who wanted to participate, the exhibition soon turned into a competition called the Diamonds USA Awards, the first given specifically to diamond designs. The judges of the highly prestigious Diamonds Awards included an incredible array of luminaries, such as actresses Kitty Carlisle and Irene Dunne, entertainment mogul Walt Disney, gossip columnist Hedda Hopper, hatmaker Lilly Daché, fashion photographer Richard Avedon, and fashion editors Nancy White of *Harper's Bazaar* and Jessica Daves of *Vogue*. With their pronounced tastes, the celebrities chose some pieces that were more for show than anything else, but they balanced these choices with genuinely ground-breaking wearable designs.

The jewelers and their prize-winning pieces were promoted in advertisements, fashion shows and magazines, museum exhibitions, and at the annual Diamond Ball, a high point of New York's social season. By the late 1950s, De Beers inaugurated a second prestigious diamond competition, the Diamonds-International Awards, to include jewelers from around the world, and formed the Diamonds-International Academy, a special honor for jewelers who won the Diamonds-International Awards at least three times. Many creative jewelers came to the fore in these competitions, which gave

On the "Today" show Betsy Palmer and Dave Garroway displayed Julius Cohen's 1958 Diamonds Award–winning jewel, a triple-tier diamond necklace featuring three pear-shaped diamonds in a platinum mounting. Jewelers who won a Diamonds Award benefited from the resulting massive media coverage.

On October 13, 1967, Richard Burton and Elizabeth Taylor flew to England on their private executive jet for the premiere of Dr. Faustus (1967) at Oxford. Taylor pinned the "Night of the Iguana" brooch to her wool cape. The heavy fabrics in style during the sixties were able to bear the weight of oversize brooches.

A bristling fishnet pattern of gold overlies the diamond scales of Elizabeth Taylor's "Night of the Iguana" brooch by Schlumberger. Pavé-set diamonds in platinum enhanced fins, tail, and ruff. A gold darting tongue, cabochon sapphire eyes, and emerald jaws give the monster a menacing expression. The 4½-inch-long jewel got its name when Richard Burton bought it for Elizabeth Taylor to wear at the premiere of the film *The Night of the Iguana* (1964), in which he starred.

them a forum to showcase their work. In essence, the Diamonds Awards replaced the big international exhibitions that had provided a venue for new jewelry styles since the nineteenth century. They fostered a supportive climate for creative jewelry and focused more attention on the jewelers than they ever could have generated on their own. Fashion critics and artistic

institutions further enhanced the prestige of these jewelers by presenting them with accolades and exhibitions.

Of all the jewelers working in the artistic mode, Jean Schlumberger was probably the most honored. He received numerous awards, including a Diamonds USA Award in 1954 and the Coty American Fashion Critics Award in 1958—the first time the fashion industry's highest honor had ever been presented to a jeweler. Exhibiting the work of creative jewelers of the sixties outside its traditional mercantile setting became commonplace during the era. Exhibitions of Schlumberger's work in Houston, New York, and Paris drew as many jewelry enthusiasts, and probably more museum figures, than had Harry Winston's Court of Jewels. In 1961, when Wildenstein & Co. in New York presented a retrospective of his jewelry, the ambassador of France, the directors of the Metropolitan Museum of Art and the Cooper Union Museum in New York, the chief curator of art at the Los Angeles County Museum of Art, and the curator of medieval and decorative arts at the Walters Art Gallery in Baltimore numbered among the patrons. Jackie Kennedy, who described Schlumberger as "a gentle and sensitive man, a brilliant designer and loyal friend," topped the list of guests and opened the show. Lenders to the exhibition included Bunny Mellon, Babe Paley, Diana Vreeland, Daisy Fellowes, Mrs. Richard Avedon, and Millicent Rogers's daughters-in-law, Mrs. Arturo Ramos and Mrs. Paul Ramos.

In the essay for the retrospective catalogue Charles Sterling, curator

Diana Vreeland talks to Jackie Kennedy at the opening of Jean Schlumberger's 1961 retrospective at Wildenstein & Co. in New York. Both women were supporters of creative jewelry in their respective spheres. As editor-in-chief of Vogue, Diana Vreeland orchestrated fashion still life photography around creative jewelry as well as including it in fashion shoots on models. She loaned her own Schlumberger trophy brooch with fringed armor, shield, and spears to the Wildenstein show. In 1976, when she was the special consultant to the Costume Institute of the Metropolitan Museum of Art, Vreeland wrote the "Postface" to the illustrated book *Jean Schlumberger*. Jackie Kennedy attended exhibitions of creative jewelers, commissioned gifts of state from David Webb, and wore her gold and enamel Schlumberger bracelets so often they were nicknamed "Jackie bracelets."

of paintings at the Louvre, expressed the sentiment of many in the artistic community: Schlumberger was more than just a jeweler, he was an artist. "Far from becoming a slave to stones and to gold, he [Schlumberger] has subjected them to deliberate and lyrical creation. Every resource offered by graphic rhythms, by the tangible interplay of volumes, by tones brought together according to unexpected harmonies—the means at the disposal of the draftsman, sculptor, painter seem to come to him effortlessly. This freedom springs from the most glorious traditions of jewelry: the settings of Byzantine smalts, the blaze of Gothic *languettes*, the smiling asymmetry of rococo. But one must strain to perceive these links with the past; for all, in this, is new and fresh. A vast culture has been assimilated unerringly in order to nurture free invention. I have not mentioned the Renaissance tradition, yet it is the one above all that Jean Schlumberger brings to life with all the spontaneity of a personal discovery. The baroque pearl which suggests a quivering body, the sea-horse with the head of a unicorn, the shell of Florentine grottoes dripping with diamond dew, the star-fish worthy of a Palissy platter—these belong to the unlimited universe of metamorphosis so dear to the manneristic XVIth century. It is surely no accident, in this as in the case of painting and sculpture, that a great artist, belonging to a time so anxious to find refuge in unreality, should turn instinctively to an art which put imagination above materialistic evocation—and the noblest of stones and metals at the service of dreams."

Schlumberger had come a long way since the beginning of his career. The son of a successful businessman who owned a silk factory in France, he came to the United States in 1930 to learn the textile business and design abstract prints. After a short period, he returned to his home in the Alsace region of France. There he worked for a publisher designing posters. Later, he moved to Paris, where he became a promoter and package designer for Lelong perfumes. It was after he was fired from this position that Schlumberger found his métier at a flea market in Paris. Legend has it that with his last three thousand francs Schlumberger purchased a tray of 120 Dresden flowers and transformed them into 120 clips. The creations were snapped up by friends and retailers, but more important, the charm of these follies traveled by word of mouth to the most innovative couturiere in Paris, Elsa Schiaparelli, who hired him to design buttons and costume jewelry in 1938. His whimsical designs for Schiaparelli—roller skate brooches, flying fish earrings, and water lily necklaces with frogs on lily pads—were so special that they were credited "Schlumberger for Schiaparelli." Her couture clientele collected them and, led by the Duchess of Kent, soon brought their precious jewelry to Schlumberger to redesign. For her trip to Australia, he made the duchess a pair of gold and diamond clips. Two American jewelry lovers, Daisy Fellowes and Mona Bismarck, encouraged Schlumberger to make the transition to precious jewelry full-time. But World War II intervened, and Schlumberger put his jewelry career on hold to serve his country in England and the Middle East for the Free French forces under General Charles de Gaulle.

After his tours of duty, Schlumberger went to New York and designed clothes for Chez Ninon until he and a friend from France, Nicolas Bongard,

A Schlumberger brooch owned by Millicent Rogers features a morganite (a rose pink beryl). It also shows the mating of white and canary diamonds set in platinum and gold respectively, a trend in creative jewelry after World War II. The asymmetrical thorny gold mount exemplifies Schlumberger's penchant for sharp-edged designs. This brooch was made in 1947, one year after Schlumberger opened his salon on 21 East Sixty-third Street in New York, and predates the jeweler's association with Tiffany.

opened a small customized jewelry firm at 21 East Sixty-third Street in 1946. Bongard brought to the partnership the creative legacy of a family that included the couturier Paul Poiret and the jeweler René Boivin. As a young man Bongard had apprenticed to his aunt Jeanne Boivin, so he added to Schlumberger's creativity a hands-on knowledge of precious gems and a thorough grasp of fine jewelry manufacturing.

After nine successful years with his own firm Schlumberger hit the big time in precious jewelry when Walter Hoving, the chairman of Tiffany & Co., invited him to become the firm's first byline designer. This move served to link the traditional New York jewelry giant with artistic jewelry, which was on the rise in popularity. Schlumberger worked in a small office at Tiffany and designed wearing a smock specially made by his friend the couturier Cristóbal Balenciaga. He sat at a collapsible traveling desk and chair, his books on eighteenth- and nineteenth-century art, plants, lace, tropical leaves, and tapestries strewn on the floor. The daily soap opera or classical music played on his portable radio.

Schlumberger's nature and fantasy theme jewels were large, and almost all his pieces had a unique frondlike gold setting that gave them—literally— a distinctive edge. The thorn and thistle aspect of the gold metalwork made Schlumberger's jewels look startling, if not dangerous. In fact, the settings for his brooches were sharp as daggers, and they punctured women's jackets, putting huge holes and rips in the linings. At least once a Schlumberger jewel drew blood. Millicent Rogers's amethyst and sapphire target brooch, shot through with nine gold arrows representing her lovers, scraped Clark Gable's chest when they were dancing. But Schlumberger clients preferred to apply bandages or reline their clothes than to give up the spiky creations.

Because Schlumberger had the reputation of an artistic jeweler who put ideas above intrinsic value, a reporter from the *New York Herald Tribune* (March 12, 1956) asked him if he liked diamonds. Schlumberger quipped, "Well, you have to, don't you. They're so expensive." Another time, when he was speaking to Dorothy Dignam, publicity representative for the advertising agency N. W. Ayer, which numbered De Beers among its clients, Schlumberger expanded on his views about the gem. He did not like geometrical shapes like baguettes, associated with Art Deco jewelry, explaining, "What can I do with those ugly little tapered ones? Women bring them in here to be remounted and what can I do with them? I wish I'd never see one again. Square cuts? I feel the same way. I hope they never come back. A woman has a bracelet in here now—all square cuts in a row. The fact that she wants to have this baguette jewelry all done over shows . . . what's beautiful about it?" Diamonds in the shape of half moons, pentagons, and triangles had an equally negative effect on him.

Schlumberger's taste in diamonds ran almost exclusively to brilliant cuts and pear shapes, as their curvilinear sides suited his organic view of design. He once explained, "I try to make everything look as if it were growing, uneven, at random, organic in motion." Taking nature as his model, he made all his pieces asymmetrical. Schlumberger achieved unevenness with circular-cut diamonds, which could be fit into asymmetrical designs, and pear shapes, which could be mounted with their tips pointing in different directions. For a snowflake, one of nature's few symmetrical creations, he turned the diamonds and the design askew. The feathery aggregates of white gems radiated from a central diamond in a raised wire setting to pavé-set diamond extensions ending in a jumble of brilliants and pear shapes in wire settings. He achieved the windblown imagery by randomly turning pear-shaped diamonds on their edges.

At the North Shore Hospital Ball in 1955, CBS executive Bill Paley sits with his wife Babe, who wears her diamond and turquoise fringe necklace by Schlumberger. According to the *New York Herald Tribune* (March 12, 1956), "Schlumberger's jewelry has started many trends that filter clear down to the budget jewelry counter. The latest is the fad for turquoises which began with a turquoise and diamond necklace designed by Schlumberger and worn by Mrs. William Paley, one of the great beauties of our time, to the Eisenhower inaugural ball."

Even though a good portion of Schlumberger's output was devoted to diamond and gold jewelry, he disapproved of wearing diamonds for diamonds' sake. "No firebombs," Schlumberger proclaimed in an interview with an N. W. Ayer representative. "No flashy and meaningless ornaments just for display. Wear one fine piece that was made for you and looks like you, don't pin a thousand dollar bill to your lapel." When designing jewels for big diamonds, he took his own advice. In 1956 he came up with a "wardrobe of settings" for the 128.51-carat Tiffany diamond: a ribbon brooch that attached to a larger necklace, a winged pendant brooch, and a daisy bracelet. All were set with white and canary diamonds to offset the brilliance of the world's largest canary diamond. Since this was the first time the Tiffany diamond (acquired by Tiffany in 1878) had ever been mounted in a jewel, Schlumberger, the designs, and the gem received considerable media attention. *Vogue* printed a spread and Audrey Hepburn posed for the press wearing the necklace with the famous black Hubert de Givenchy sheath she had on in the first scene of the movie *Breakfast at Tiffany's* (1961).

The high-profile coverage Schlumberger enjoyed as Tiffany's artist-in-residence helped pave the way for other artistic jewelers. Like Schlumberger, many of them initially gained exposure to a broad public as winners of one of the De Beers Diamonds Awards.

Parisian jeweler Pierre Sterlé won the Diamonds-International Award three years in a row, beginning in 1953. His all-diamond jewelry displayed a classical rigor and appreciation for fine formal designs with a modern twist. He used an even mix of circular- and baguette-cut diamonds in his jewelry. One of Sterlé's unique takes on the formal diamond necklace was a looped row of staggered baguette cuts that merged at the back with a line of circular cuts. He wrapped a standard bracelet of four rows of circular-cut diamonds with a triple row of baguette cuts, making it unusually broad. A series of abstract diamond brooches drew inspiration from a bird's outstretched wings. Sterlé lined the bottom of the aerodynamic motif with baguettes and paved the top with circular cuts, giving the piece an inside-out appearance.

Sterlé's familiarity with traditional diamond designs came from an early exposure to jewelry. His uncle, who was a jeweler, became his guardian after his father died during World War I. At a young age Sterlé became an apprentice and grew up learning about fine jewelry in the family business on the rue de Castiglione in Paris. He began his own firm in 1934 at age twenty-nine and manufactured jewelry and small luxury items for Boucheron, Chaumet, Ostertag, and Puiforcat. Sterlé's skills at the bench were so fine he personally trained his foremen Deschamps and Gilbert Diltoer.

When the economy took an upswing in the 1950s, Sterlé's name became well known, not only through his award-winning diamond jewels but also from his collaborations with some of the best couturiers in Paris, starting with Jacques Fath. The sight of Fath pinning a rose petal to his wife's dress inspired Sterlé to create a clip with a white rose petal of pavé-set diamonds against a red rose petal of rubies pierced by a baguette-cut diamond pin. In another instance Sterlé's diamond arrow clips underscored the theme of Fath's new arrow line. Fath showed the jewels on his daytime and evening dresses. Sterlé also worked with Balmain, Dior, and Rochas. Of all the couturiers, Sterlé most admired Madame Alix Grès, noting an affinity between his jewelry and the clean line of her clothes with their characteristic Hellenic drape.

The originality of Sterlé's jewels and their alignment with fashion attracted royalty from around the world who wanted to update their collections. The maharani of Baroda added the Frenchman to her list of favorite Continental jewelers. The wife of King Farouk had Sterlé freshen up some of the Egyptian crown jewels. And the Begum Aga Khan commissioned Sterlé to mount her Persian turquoise in a diamond bib necklace.

Sterlé's most famous concoction was a series of bird brooches with flut-

In 1956 Schlumberger designed a "wardrobe of settings" for the 128.51-carat Tiffany diamond. His drawings for the gem were unveiled in a *Vogue* editorial of November 15, 1956, that explained, "each of the three uses mainly platinum and white diamonds—to offset, with their coolness, the Tiffany diamond's golden brilliance."

For a press reception Audrey Hepburn wore the Givenchy dress from the movie *Breakfast at Tiffany's* (1961) and Schlumberger's canary and white diamond woven ribbon necklace with the Tiffany diamond as the centerpiece. The three-dimensionality of the ruffled diamond ribbons was typical of Schlumberger work. Through her charming portrayal of Holly Go-lightly, Audrey Hepburn became permanently linked with the jewelry firm. Indeed, her fondness for Tiffany's in the movie turned it into the one jewelry store in New York that has become a tourist attraction.

Polished labradorite forms the body of Sterlé's bird brooch, and gold loop-in-loop chains make up the fluttering plumage. Diamonds mounted in platinum enhance every part of the jewel from the head and beak to the wing tips and tail.

tering plumage composed of loop-in-loop chains (called fil d'ange). The gold motif had a look as old as Cleopatra, whose bracelets had inspired the jeweler during a visit to the Cairo Museum. For the birds' bodies, Sterlé used a variety of materials, including semiprecious stones such as labradorite, malachite, amethyst, and coral. No matter how far afield he ventured in materials, Sterlé almost always included diamonds on his birds. Circular cuts mounted in platinum defined the V-shaped tails, wing tips, beaks, and caps of the swift brooches and amplified the riches of his tropical birds, outlining wings and defining eyes, beaks, and breasts. Sterlé's diamond flights of fancy became his signature jewel and secured his place in the ranks of creative jewelers.

Like Pierre Sterlé, New York jeweler Julius Cohen came from a family of manufacturing jewelers and won several Diamonds Awards. He began his career in 1929 working at the bench and later traveling and selling jewelry for his uncle's manufacturing firm, Oscar Heyman & Brothers. When Cohen left the family enclave in 1942, he joined Harry Winston as a salesman. Among other duties, he toured the country with the Court of Jewels to promote and educate people about diamonds. After thirteen years with Winston, Cohen opened his own jewelry salon, Julius Cohen Jeweler, next

New York personality Maggie McNellis wears her "Flame of Gold" necklace by Julius Cohen at a 1957 Diamonds Award presentation in New York. The center stone of the necklace is a 28.86-carat canary diamond set in a burst of diamond flames. The motif is repeated with twelve smaller pear-shaped diamonds surrounded by baguette-cut diamond sparks on an undulating tapered baguette-cut diamond necklace. Gold and platinum are both used in the mounting.

to the Stork Club at 17 East Fifty-third Street in New York, selling designs that emphasized nature and whimsical follies. Though his work contrasted directly with the abstract formal display of gems at Harry Winston, he carried over the master's great love of big diamonds, explaining to a reporter, "When you're in the presence of a large, beautiful stone, you have a certain amount of awe and respect for it. There's no fear at all. Your experience brings you to a point of appreciation. You don't think of it as being worth $400,000. You are aware it's a special thing that nature has made. That is the extraordinary thing about it. Being able to enjoy it is a result of man. It is found as a pebble, a rough stone. It takes man's vision and courage to start cutting it and envision how it can look."

Cohen was the only creative jeweler who consistently incorporated big diamonds into his pieces. In 1957, working with Ann Samols, one of his designers, Cohen conceived a necklace with a fiery theme inspired by a 28.86-carat canary diamond. The huge stone was mounted in a blaze of diamond flames suspended by an undulating line of tapered baguettes punctuated by pear shapes in sparks of baguettes. Named the "Flame of Gold," the necklace won an award at the 1957 Diamonds-International competition before making its way into the private collection of MGM film star Greer Garson.

A pair of closely matched portrait canary diamonds (thinly cut diamonds with two large, flat tables) weighing a total of 20.55 carats triggered the idea for Cohen's 1958 "Phoenix" jewel. The unusually shaped diamonds formed the wings of a three-dimensional pavé-set diamond bird with an elaborate tail of canary and white diamonds and emeralds. The "Phoenix" could be worn as a clip or attached to a necklace with scattered round diamonds set in platinum and diamonds set in gold motifs. Like many of the creative jewelers, Cohen preferred gold in his formal pieces, explaining to Ann Phinney Mundy for her syndicated article "Courage, Artistry Required in Jewelry Design," "because I feel it is a much more satisfactory metal, and it's warmer in color. But we will use platinum all through our jewelry to make a contrast."

One of the most publicized gems Cohen mounted was the Great Chrysanthemum. The gem came from a 198.28-carat soft honey-colored diamond rough Cohen bought in 1963. He oversaw the cutting process and made all the decisions along the way to achieve a 104.15-carat pear shape that became the pendant in an oversize floral necklace of 50 oval, 96 marquise, and 264 baguette-cut diamonds enriched by a gold and platinum mounting.

Cohen's extraordinary combination of creative designs and impressive diamonds made him the darling of the Diamonds Award jurors year after year. In 1957 he won six Diamonds USA Awards, in 1958 he won seven, and in 1959 he won nine Diamonds-International Awards, a trend he continued year in and year out. As in his earlier days with Winston's Court of Jewels, Cohen made the exhibition circuit. One of the most important shows he participated in was the 1967 exhibition at the Smithsonian Institution honoring Diamonds Award–winning jewels from the Diamonds-International Academy. Cohen shared the spotlight with his work on opening night when he escorted Mrs. Clark Thompson, wife of the representative from Texas, through the galleries. The *Washington Post* (February 9, 1967) reported, "On

A branch brooch made by Julius Cohen in 1968 shows a platinum and diamond stem and gold sculptured motifs sprinkled with diamonds.

Opposite: The pavé-set diamond "Phoenix" brooch by Julius Cohen featured in *Harper's Bazaar* (November 1958) displays unusual portrait canary diamond wings separated by fifty-two round canary diamonds on the bird's back. The extravagant tail has white and canary marquise-cut diamonds and pear-shaped emeralds. Highlighting the supporting gold branch is a cinnamon briolette diamond. On completion of the "Phoenix," Cohen's client arranged for its eventual placement in a Texas museum.

New flight of the jeweler's art: a bird whose plumage is all rare stones. Two perfectly matched canary diamonds form wings; the body is feathered in white diamonds; the tail is of emeralds, white and yellow diamonds. It hovers on a golden bough fruited with a briolette diamond. From Julius Cohen. Traina-Norell's enchanting dress is of Chantilly lace in a warm golden color, blown out from a yoke into a froth of a flounce. Under it: its own fitted white satin slip. At Lord and Taylor; Julius Garfinckel, Washington; Dayton's, Minneapolis; I. Magnin. Lilly Daché hat; Hansen gloves; Christian Dior stockings. Shoes by Evins. The earrings by Julius Cohen.

WILLIAM HELBURN

Mrs. Thompson's right hand were an emerald-cut diamond ring and a diamond bracelet. On her left hand was a ring that was a cluster of diamonds, and a diamond bracelet. At her right elbow was jeweler Julius Cohen of New York."

The oldest among the group of creative jewelers, Seaman Schepps was seventy-three when he won his first Diamonds Award in 1954. In the first two decades of the century Schepps had traveled back and forth between New York, Los Angeles, and San Francisco with his wife Nell, opening and closing antique jewelry shops. After the stock-market crash Nell persuaded Schepps to concentrate on his own designs at his shop on Madison Avenue. Fashion was in flux, and she felt his unusual jewelry would attract attention. Schepps quickly found a following for his oversize, bulbous, colorful, and quirky work.

With the postwar madness for diamonds, Schepps used the gem like no other jeweler, mixing it freely with outrageous materials such as branch coral, baroque pearls, hunks of crystal, wood, lapis lazuli, and bric-a-brac. These materials gave his pieces a wildly asymmetrical aspect. If clients complained about the off-kilter quality of a pair of earrings, Schepps waved aside their concern, saying, "Why do you want each earring to exactly match the other one? You've got your whole head in between." Schepps did not even consider making matching suites of jewelry. Like all the creative jewelers, he encouraged his clients to combine their pieces.

Some of his more spectacular diamond-set jewels won prizes at the Diamonds Awards competitions throughout the fifties and sixties, and he became a member of the Diamonds-International Academy. Most of his award-winning pieces took their themes from nature—flowers, animals, fish—but some used abstract forms with scribbles of diamonds. Schepps's first Diamonds Award honored a brooch with two carved coral goldfish mounted in a swirl of diamond and turquoise waves. He won another for a simple choker with alternating S-scrolls of diamonds, turquoise, and gold.

Schepps's color schemes came from an eclectic group of sources. Soft pastels stemmed from his love of the work of eighteenth-century French painter Jean-Honoré Fragonard, which he studied at the Frick Museum in New York. The clashing colors of the Ballets Russes and Paul Poiret remained in the jeweler's memory from his travels in Paris during the teens and surfaced in bolder palettes. The nineteenth-century flower paintings of Henri Fantin-Latour also influenced his color choices.

Although Schepps appreciated the fine arts, he was no museum snob. He frequented flea markets and pawn shops in search of oddments and junk to be recycled for their materials or incorporated into jewelry just as they were. The Asian culture Schepps imbibed in the Chinatowns of Los Angeles and San Francisco held an ongoing fascination for the jeweler. In 1955 he went on a trip with his wife to the Far East, where he fell completely under the spell of the exotic. The couple extended their tour in Hong Kong for three months, visiting museums, temples, and, of course, merchants, where Schepps ferreted out coral, jade, and ivory carvings. For a fiftieth-anniversary present to his wife, Schepps set one of his finds, a white coral figurine

A 1957 Diamonds Award–winning jewel, the "Goddess of Heaven" brooch by Seaman Schepps features a slender white coral figurine, surrounded by swirls of diamonds set in white gold and single diamond and pearl accents. A platinum and diamond element with millegrain detail from a jewel made around 1900 makes up the headdress.

representing an Oriental goddess of heaven, in a diamond and gold brooch. The jewel won Schepps another Diamonds Award.

Schepps's original style with diamonds endeared him to the likes of actress Lauren Bacall, television host and former Miss America Jinx Falkenberg, and Blanche Knopf of the publishing family. Other jewelers interested in innovation kept an eye on Seaman Schepps's bravado. David Webb, a young creative jeweler, was so entranced by Schepps's daring juxtapositions that he frequently lingered at the display window. One day he stood there so long that Schepps himself came outside and asked, "David, would you like a chair?"

David Webb eventually became a top creative jeweler. Like Schlumberger, Sterlé, Cohen, and Schepps, Webb received multiple Diamonds Awards, and he was the second fine jeweler to win the Coty Award. David Webb captured the fashion industry honor in 1964 for his animal kingdom jewelry. Snakes, unicorns, frogs, dragons, and lions curled into wraparound rings and bracelets with gleaming enamel surfaces studded with gems. Their bodies gave form to earrings and brooches. Some of Webb's ideas for these jewels came from classical Greek jewelry, like the solid gold bracelets with animal finials from the fourth century B.C. Webb analyzed Greek gold regularly at New York's Metropolitan Museum of Art. He also cited the Medici Collection and the south German and northern Italian schools of goldsmithing as sources of inspiration.

Although Webb mined the wealth of archaeology and art history, his results were completely contemporary. The large scale of his jewels held its own with the brightly colored multiple-stripe mod outfits worn by jet-set women who spent much of their time in airports between parties, vacations, and work. His animal jewels, made to be worn with daytime attire, offered a spirited alternative to formal diamond jewelry. In fact, his zoo was so reasonably priced for precious jewelry that Harry Winston reportedly sent his clients to David Webb for their casual fare. The King of Diamonds regarded Webb's jewels, with their brightly colored enamels and diamond accents, as a short step up from costume jewelry.

The rage for Webb animal jewelry began with his first suite of black and white striped enamel zebras sprinkled with diamonds. According to the *New York Herald Tribune* (May 27, 1964), "One of the first takers for the zebra bracelet was Mrs. Richard (Dorothy) Rogers. She was followed quickly by *Vogue* editor-in-chief Diana Vreeland, Anne Ford and decorator Melanie Kahane. The enamel bracelets come in limited editions of ten and the zebras are virtually sold out. It's too expensive, David Webb explains, to make a mold for a single bracelet. Though some of his collectors are already muttering about buying the mold so they can have a one-of-a-kind jewel, none of them have come up yet with the grand, throw-away gesture."

The gem-set enamel jewels have a hand-wrought quality that evolved from David Webb's background of handwork and artistic training. He grew up in Asheville, North Carolina, and discovered his passion for gems and jewelry at age nine, pounding out pewter and copper ashtrays at a WPA metal craft school. Webb's father was a jeweler and his grandfather a drafts-

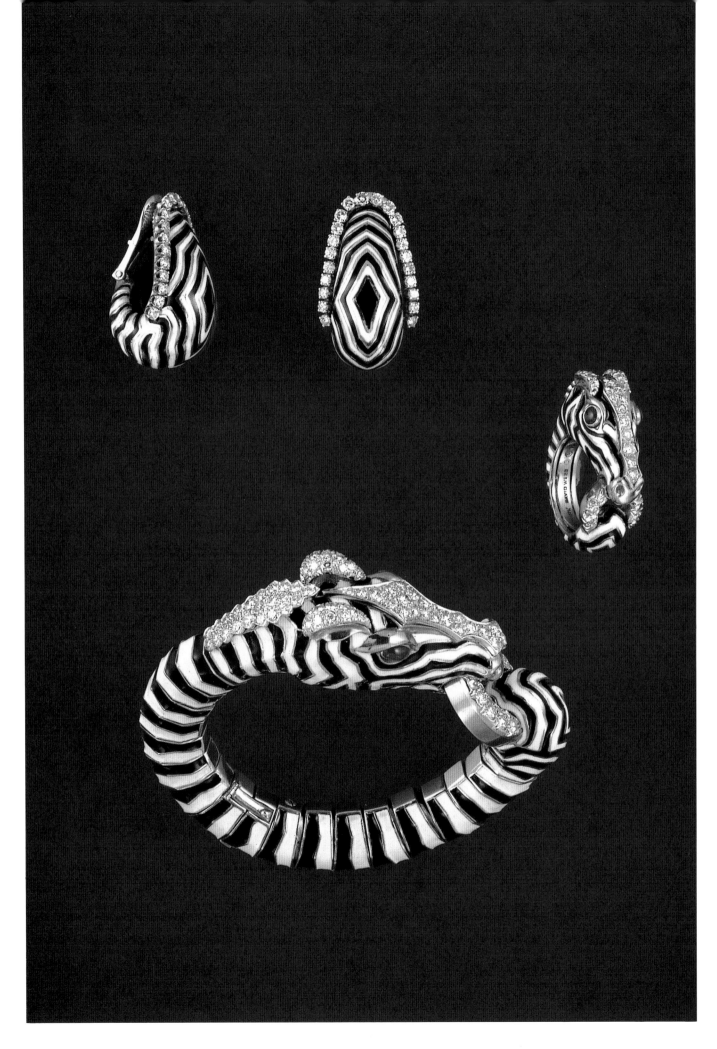

Diana Vreeland's zebras were among the first designs in David Webb's animal kingdom series, which won him the prestigious Coty American Fashion Critics Award in 1964. Black and white enamel and gold zebras form a ring (on the right) and a bracelet (below) with diamond manes set in platinum and cabochon ruby eyes. The earrings (on the upper left) feature zebra stripes and diamond accents.

A pair of enamel, diamond, and gold frog brooches by David Webb made an imaginative still life for a De Beers advertisement. The 1969 ad illustrates the creative jewelry supported by the De Beers–sponsored Diamonds Awards, and the text summarizes a change in attitude toward the gem: "A surprise look at what once was strictly a grande dame gem. No more. Diamonds can be kicky as frog's eyes, classic as ear drops or anything your pleasure or purse desires. The one thing that hasn't changed is the thrill you get from wearing them. A diamond is for now."

man and metalworker. At age fourteen, Webb learned goldsmithing and gem setting from his uncle. After high school Webb skipped further education in favor of a summer course at Penland School of Handicrafts in North Carolina. At age seventeen he set off for New York, where he became a jeweler's apprentice in the heart of the jewelry district. Four years later, he had his own business—David Webb, Inc.—with a partner, Nina Silberstein. Their timing could not have been better. In this postwar period, the demand for formal diamond jewels reached its peak.

Since David Webb could not compete with the capital investment in fine diamonds of Harry Winston and Van Cleef & Arpels, he made less expensive trendy diamond jewels for private clients who liked to be on the cutting edge. They brought Webb their diamonds and commissioned him to reset them every three or four years. Webb was happy to work with the older diamond shapes his clients inherited, such as the old-mine and rose cuts. He did not recommend recutting because he felt the old diamonds had an interesting light. He backed rose cuts in polished white gold to heighten their twinkle. (White gold was a less expensive alternative to platinum. The bleaching properties of nickel with small amounts of silver and zinc, when alloyed with fine gold, turned the metal white. However, the nickel-gold

De Beers Consolidated Mines, Ltd.

Frog pins by David Webb. Your jeweler can show you many exciting diamond pieces priced from about $200.

A surprise look at what once was strictly a grande dame gem. No more. Diamonds can be kicky as frog's eyes, classic as ear drops or anything your pleasure or purse desires. The one thing that hasn't changed is the thrill you get from wearing them. A diamond is for now.

alloy, while very white, was extremely hard and lacked the ductility of platinum.) For off-color, slightly yellowish diamonds that were nicknamed "blonde," he devised yellow gold mountings to make the diamonds appear whiter. These jewels won him a following of notables, including the legendary vaudeville singer Sophie Tucker and Doris Day, who flaunted her Webb jewelry in the movies *Pillow Talk* (1959) and *Midnight Lace* (1960). Susan Hayward wore $1,150,000 worth of Webb jewelry in *Back Street* (1961), and within a week of the film's debut the entire collection sold out.

When David Webb debuted the animal kingdom jewelry, he rocketed to superstar status. This sudden celebrity brought an unwelcome kind of attention: costume jewelers, and some precious jewelers, began imitating his pieces. In order to separate himself from his imitators, Webb also made objects. Notable among these were gifts of state commissioned by First Lady Jackie Kennedy for visiting dignitaries that featured native American gemstones. For President Fanfani of Italy, Webb simply wrapped a chunk of Arizona malachite in gold rope. One of David Webb's clients bequeathed two of his objects to the Philadelphia Museum of Art: a gold frog with emerald eyes and diamond toenails and a gold bonsai tree decorated with diamonds and planted in a gold bamboo bucket. Webb's sculptural work was exhibited frequently, and more than once he was proclaimed the new Cellini.

Bridging the gap between his sculpture and jewelry, Webb created compacts, lighters, and clocks as functional versions of his objects. One of the most charming in his forty-piece collection of 1964 was a gold tortoise compact with pavé-set diamond head, feet, and tail and a real tortoise's shell for the body. While Webb's enamel and diamond animal kingdom jewelry came across as casual in a period of glittering high-carat weights, his objects, with their individuality and liberal use of diamonds, looked extravagant.

Pavé-set diamond head, feet, and tail protrude from a real tortoise's shell that forms the cover of a gold compact by David Webb. The slow-moving creature watches the world with emerald eyes.

Although Webb spoke of finding historical inspiration for his menagerie, he tipped his hat to one contemporary jeweler, telling *Vogue* (March 15, 1964), "It's completely Toussaint's influence, of course—she is the inspiration of us all." David Webb was referring to Jeanne Toussaint, the artistic director of Cartier, and the great cats she let loose in the postwar period. The gem-encrusted beasts—primarily panthers or tigers—wrapped around wrists, dangled as earrings, and leapt across lapels. The distinctive jewels became Cartier's signature pieces of the fifties and sixties.

The panther was not the first signature look Toussaint devised for Cartier. She had made a career of dreaming up original ideas for the firm. In 1910, at age twenty-three, Jeanne Toussaint joined Cartier in Paris. Her

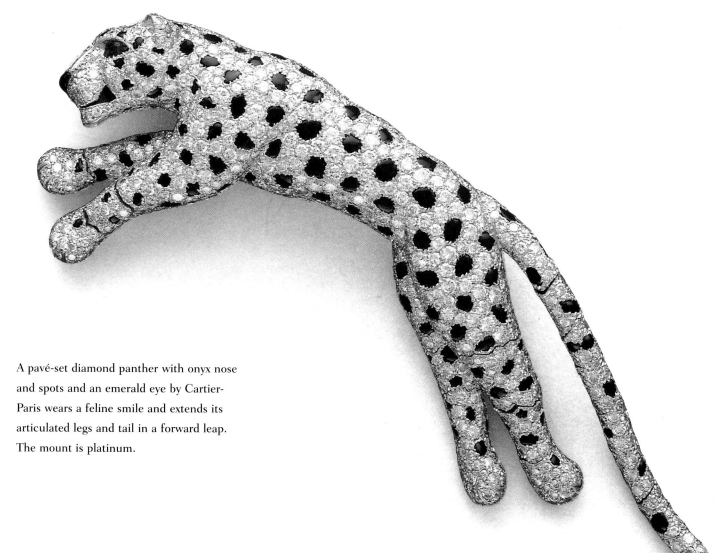

A pavé-set diamond panther with onyx nose
and spots and an emerald eye by Cartier-
Paris wears a feline smile and extends its
articulated legs and tail in a forward leap.
The mount is platinum.

job began as a thinly veiled excuse to be close to her lover, Louis Cartier. But
Toussaint had a natural artistic finesse that led Cecil Beaton to write in
Vogue (January 1, 1965) half a century later that she "revolutionized jewellery," and "invented and kept alive the Cartier style." As creative director
of Department S in the twenties, Toussaint accentuated contemporary fashion in the small items the department handled. For example, she purchased
embroidered materials from China and Persia for handbags to go with
dresses by Jean Patou and her friend Coco Chanel, using frames, clasps, and
pulls encrusted with all sorts of precious stones and, sometimes, a mini-
watch as well. Having performed miracles with the department, Toussaint
was promoted to creative director of luxury jewelry in 1933 when this area,
the firm's most prestigious, found itself in jeopardy due to the Depression.
Toussaint's penchant for Oriental splendor surfaced in Indian-inspired jewelry. It incorporated beautiful but unusual stones, elements from actual
Indian finery, and tassels and clusters of diamonds, precious beads, and
pearls. Even without using the more costly faceted precious gems, the jewelry produced a grand effect and proved to be one of the great styles of the
century. The best-known series, now called "fruit salad" or "tutti frutti," displayed carved precious Indian gems punctuated by diamonds, a confection
that clients found delectable. Cole Porter commissioned a clip brooch and

two bracelets for his wife Linda and Singer sewing machine heiress Daisy Fellowes owned a multitiered "fruit-salad" necklace and matching earrings.

Toussaint oversaw all phases of jewelry production at Cartier, from the first ink and gouache designs to the final polishing. Louis Cartier advised her not to learn to draw. She complied, explaining, "this inability enables me to criticize the work of others." The "fruit salad" series was dished up with gifted designer Charles Jacqueau, and the legendary panther series was refined with designer Peter Lemarchand.

"Panther" was Louis Cartier's amorous nickname for Toussaint. The sinuous, beautiful, but dangerous feline appears in Cartier creations as early as 1914. The brood multiplied at midcentury, when Toussaint unleashed felines displaying glossy diamond hides with sapphire or black onyx spots.

Barbara Hutton's suite of tiger jewelry includes a pair of earrings with canary diamonds shading to white diamonds and black onyx stripes and emerald eyes. The gems are set in gold. Suspended like the fifteenth-century motif of the Golden Fleece, the beasts' heads, legs, and tails are articulated. Hutton's tigers from Cartier-Paris were designed under the direction of Jeanne Toussaint. The brooch was made in 1957 and the earrings in 1961.

Woolworth heiress Barbara Hutton arrived in New York on the ocean liner United States, accompanied by eligible New York bachelor Philip Van Rensselaer. Pinned to Hutton's jacket is her onyx and canary and white diamond tiger brooch by Cartier-Paris.

The supple body of the panthers shaped rings, bangles, earrings, stickpins, and brooches. Later, Toussaint added tigers to the series. Their tawny yellow bodies gave her an opportunity to employ canary diamonds. She achieved variation in color by shading the bright yellow gems with white diamonds, a masterful mix of stones, and employed black onyx for the stripes. The dangling beasts in brooches and earrings imitated the sheepskin posture of the Golden Fleece emblem made for an order of knights founded by Philip the Good of Burgundy in the fifteenth century.

Toussaint's costly great cats prompted some of the richest women in the world to go big-game hunting. Nina Dyer, wife of Prince Sadruddin Aga Khan, took home a litter of four jewels. Daisy Fellowes, always on the cusp of Toussaint's breaking jewelry styles, commissioned a panther brooch. The Duchess of Windsor had panthers in all shapes and sizes as well as a few tigers. And "Poor Little Rich Girl" Barbara Hutton, the Woolworth heiress, had a family of tigers.

One of the most remarkable pieces produced under Toussaint's direction in the late sixties, the twilight of her career, was a snake necklace designed by Gabriel Raton for Maria Felix, the Mexican film star. The dimensions of the snake, the setting and arrangement of the diamonds, the patterning of the enamel, and the well-devised diamond peg clasp presented any number of problems and details to be solved and fine-tuned. Felix brought Cartier hundreds of her own diamonds and the firm added around 1,800 more to the collection. The barbaric quality of the late sixties jewel showed how Toussaint could keep up a flow of innovative ideas to match the tenor of the times.

Though Toussaint was not a byline designer at Cartier (the firm never had byline designers for precious jewelry) and she never entered a Diamonds Awards competition—though she certainly would have won several—she was the matriarch of the creative jewelers. She had always treated jewelry as an art form, inspired by exotic civilizations, history, and art, telling *Vogue* (March 15, 1964), "I live in museums."

In the mid-fifties, when the styles of Harry Winston and Van Cleef & Arpels featuring medium-size pear-shaped, marquise, and baguette-cut diamonds clustered in groups and arranged in rows dominated precious jewelry design, the creative jewelers—Jean Schlumberger, Pierre Sterlé, Julius Cohen, Seaman Schepps, David Webb, and Jeanne Toussaint—changed the way people viewed diamond jewelry from formal decorations to artistic creations. The creative jewelers integrated diamonds into pieces with enamel and any number of semiprecious stones, as well as more unusual materials, and they contrasted white diamonds set in platinum with canary diamonds set in gold. The critical praise heaped on these jewelers for their original work affected the course of design, making a unique individual style a key factor in the success of the future jeweler.

CHAPTER 9

DIAMOND MINIMALISM

The role of diamonds in jewelry changed dramatically during the 1970s. Diamond jewels with clean lines replaced sculptural pieces with representational subjects and whimsical flourishes. Two jewelers, Bulgari and Elsa Peretti, a byline designer at Tiffany, became synonymous with the era. Both created individual diamond styles that could take a woman from the office into the evening and then some. Working within the restrictions of a bad economy, these jewelers shifted the emphasis of design from luxury to minimalism.

The postwar period of prosperity had ended in 1968, when the index of the New York Stock Exchange halted its upward swing and began to fall. The value of common stocks decreased by approximately 42 percent during the seventies. In 1973 Middle East emirates shook the foundations of world markets and personal finances by cutting production and raising the price of crude oil, causing a highly inflated economy.

When Bulgari opened its New York branch at the Pierre Hotel, the first question from a *New York Times* (December 14, 1971) reporter concerned the soft dollar. Gianni Bulgari replied, "No, I'm not worried about America's economic situation." The Italian firm pared down styles and created pieces that were jewelry counterparts to the simplified fashions of the period. Gianni Bulgari made the goals of the firm utterly clear when he told *Women's Wear Daily* (November 19, 1970), "We want to do important things casually so they're not just worn for special occasions."

As third-generation jewelers, the Bulgari brothers, Gianni, Paolo, and Nicola, all in their twenties and thirties, managed to balance the about-face in fashion with an abiding veneration for craftsmanship and their firm's long history. Their Greek grandfather, Sotirio Boulgaris, left his homeland in the mid-nineteenth century and settled in Rome, where he dealt in silver and trinkets from a *bancarella* (a rolling cart) on the Spanish Steps. By 1905, Sotirio and his sons Constantino and Giorgio had a jewelry firm on the Via Condotti, where they sold precious gems and jewelry and some crown jewels. As their reputation grew, so did their international clientele, who always included a stop at Bulgari on their itineraries. Supposedly Mrs. Cornelius Vanderbilt Whitney, after receiving Empress Eugénie's pearl necklace as a

Pavé-set diamonds cover gold "Open Heart," "Bean," and "Teardrop" pendants by Elsa Peretti, who varied the look of her designs by making them in diamonds and gold as well as silver.

For a 1972 advertisement featured in *Vogue*, Bulgari presented its new jewels. The brooch at upper left is reminiscent of the "temple of love" brooches of the twenties, except that the diamond, crystal, and gold facade of the Italian firm's jewel is far more intricate. Pavé-set diamonds make vivid geometric patterns against dark semiprecious stones in the jewels at right and left; the pared-down look is a bold and original update of Art Deco. A diamond and pearl brooch at the bottom rounds out the selection.

Actress Jessica Lange appeared on the cover of *Interview* (April 1979) wearing baguette-cut diamond earrings with a square-cut canary diamond and a rectangular-cut emerald by Bulgari. Bulgari particularly liked the baguette-cut diamond. The geometric gem matched the bold, clean lines of its jewelry. Jessica Lange frequently wore Bulgari jewelry in movies and publicity appearances. Her cover image on *Interview* publicized the movie *All That Jazz* (1979), in which she appeared. Three years earlier, when Lange revived Fay Wray's role in the remake of *King Kong* (1976), she spent most of the movie clutched in the fist of an oversize gorilla—but Bulgari still received a screen credit for her jewelry.

gift from her husband, went to Bulgari to browse for pearls to replace two missing from the jewel. The family opened the vault and produced the original pearls from the necklace on the spot.

Over the years Giorgio concentrated on design, traveling from Rome to Paris to take in artistic events like the Ballets Russes and the 1925 "Exposition des Arts Décoratifs." Constantino became the scholar of the family, writing the definitive tome on silver, *Argentieri gemmari e orafi d'Italie*, in five volumes. The magnificent gem-set jewels in which the firm specialized attracted some of the world's most discriminating jewelry collectors over the years. During the twenties Hollywood star Kay Francis bought her Art Deco jewelry from Bulgari. Princess Grace of Monaco and Merle Oberon patronized the firm at midcentury for formal wear.

When Giorgio became ill in the mid-sixties, his three sons assumed the responsibilities of running the family firm. One of the first things they did was open up a series of branches outside Italy. At the time of Bulgari's expansion, the status jewelry had enjoyed during the fifties and early sixties had fallen to a low. Only too aware of the problems, Gianni Bulgari told *W* (November 15, 1974), "Our aim is to restore the dignity of jewelry. People should be induced to believe that possessing a beautiful piece of jewelry is as esthetically rewarding as having a painting. The business will only survive if it shows tremendous creativity and imagination—if it presents itself as a form of art."

The Bulgari aesthetic showed an extraordinary knowledge of the history of jewelry. The firm managed to transform motifs and styles from previous eras without any suggestion of revivalist regurgitation. For many of its seventies gem-set jewels, Bulgari drew on the strong principles of Art Deco. To update the flat, geometric forms, the firm stripped them of extraneous details and blew up the scale. For a necklace of large circle motifs with an oversize circle pendant, strips of black onyx alternated with diamonds. The palette of black and white carried out in onyx and diamonds recalled the white Art Deco era of the early 1930s, when it was chic to wear all-diamond jewelry with all-black attire.

On the subjects of shapes and diamonds, Gianni Bulgari told the *New York Post* (September 1, 1970) "Inside Fashion" reporter Eugénie Sheppard, "Women are tired of curves. Even in stones they prefer rectangular-cut baguettes." Almost single-handedly Bulgari made the baguette and geometric diamond fashionable again. They recreated Art Deco chandelier earrings by tripling the number of vertically set baguette-cut diamonds and topping them off with emerald-cut stones.

With its gold line, Bulgari created a sensation by taking antique Roman coins and intaglios and setting them in heavy white and yellow gold chains and coiled bracelets. In an interview with *Town & Country*, Nicola could barely contain his enthusiasm: "Look at this! Coins have immortalized every important person in history. Caesar. Augustus. Henry VIII. Here—three coins of Nero—bronze, silver and gold, set in gold. So simple. So important. Very Bulgari!" Before the coins were mounted, they were researched in

Ernest Babelon's classic text *Roman Coins*, published in 1885. Because these jewels were made in numerous variations, diamonds entered the designs in different ways. Pavé-set diamonds covered and flanked the bezel settings of coin and intaglio mounts, and they were applied generously to the white and yellow gold links. The successful mixing of antique elements that had not been seen in jewelry since the turn of the century with diamonds and modern gold chains exemplified Bulgari's feel for the old and new.

Bulgari continuously worked with diamonds on both its coin and intaglio chains and its gem-set jewels. As Nicola Bulgari maintained, "The diamond is the common denominator of jewelry. It ties all the things together. It is fundamental." The pure sparkle and whiteness of diamonds matched the simplicity of pieces destined to be worn with the tunics, turtlenecks, and pantsuits that were the rage for both daytime and evening attire.

When Bulgari officially opened its New York branch in 1971, it had a slew of parties to welcome clients, such as Lyn Revson, Nan Kempner, Cheray Duchin, Mitzi Newhouse, and fashion arbiters, including *Harper's Bazaar* editor Nancy White and fashion designer Halston. Bulgari also invited some competitors. Claude Arpels of Van Cleef & Arpels was astonished by the minimal presentation, with houseplants instead of jewelry serving as table centerpieces. The young jewelers had even pinned a brooch to the fabric walls of their Pierre Hotel boutique, which they liked to call a studio. Reporting for the *Chicago Tribune* (December 27, 1971), Bill Cunningham playfully wondered "if this might develop into an important new trend—displaying precious jewels instead of wearing them out at night." Walter Hoving of Tiffany, who also attended, told the *New York Times* (December 14, 1971), "I'm just tickled to death. We'll all do much more business because they're here. This makes New York the center of the jewelry business in the world. We have everything now that Paris and Rome do. If I thought they'd hurt my business, I would never have come to lunch."

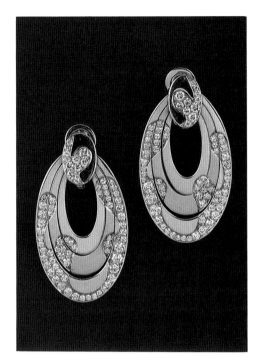

Casual but elegant, Lyn Revson's triple-hoop gold oval earrings, made by Bulgari in the seventies, are splashed with circular-cut diamond designs.

At the 1971 opening of the Bulgari boutique in the Pierre Hotel in New York, Lyn Revson, wife of Charles Revson of Revlon, was photographed by the *New York Times* looking at a case of Bulgari jewelry. Around her neck she wears a long gold Bulgari chain with a fourth-century B.C. coin depicting Athena and Pegasus and ten smaller silver coins, statere of Corinto from the fourth and third centuries B.C.

Lyn Revson's coin necklace by Bulgari features "The Penny of Scotland" (1797), with a profile of Adam Smith, in a white and yellow gold mounting accented by a series of baguette-cut diamonds. The coin pendant is suspended by a geometric hinge from a necklace of faceted citrine beads.

Walter Hoving, however, had no intention of letting Bulgari, with its contemporary style, upstage Tiffany in that department. A couple of years after Bulgari arrived in New York, Hoving enlisted the second byline designer in the firm's history to keep the giant jeweler up to par with changing styles.

After Walter Hoving asked Elsa Peretti to join Tiffany in 1974, one of the first areas to feel her touch was diamond jewelry design. Because she had worked previously with large silver forms, she found the transition to diamonds daunting at first. "I was shy about working with precious stones," Peretti commented. "I'd never done it before. The personality of even a .3 carat is strong." Remembering the beauty of her Aunt Nina's wedding ring, a 1-carat diamond set in silver with a gold band, Peretti overcame her trepidation. For her first diamond jewel she delicately sprinkled twelve small diamonds set in gold collets along a chain at uneven intervals. On seeing the design of gems set on a thirty-six-inch chain, Halston spontaneously named it "Diamonds by the Yard." Peretti varied the jewel by choosing different lengths and carat weights. The simplest version had a single diamond and sold at Tiffany for eighty-nine dollars.

With "Diamonds by the Yard," Elsa Peretti created a diamond jewel within the reach of a woman on a budget. It also proved a popular diamond jewelry choice among the "Ultrasuaves," trendsetters who wore Halston clothes, especially his Ultrasuede numbers, from head to toe. As editor-in-chief of *Vogue*, Grace Mirabella made a statement on the times—and jewelry—by wearing mostly Halston and Peretti after she replaced Diana Vreeland and set about reconstructing the image of the fashion magazine. Elsa Peretti and Halston presented "Diamonds by the Yard" as a wedding present to Liza Minnelli, who reveled in her sparkling strands. The jewel also appeared on a model on the cover of *Newsweek* (April 4, 1977) to prepare the readers for the article about young designers entitled "Jewelry's New Dazzle." Referring to the design, Peretti said simply, "There is nothing more pretty than a little diamond on a chain."

After the overwhelmingly positive reception of "Diamonds by the Yard," Peretti applied the gem to several of her signature motifs. For the "Open Heart" and "Bean" pendants, she spread diamonds across their curved surfaces, working with Tiffany master craftsman Carlos Lucyk. Together they came up with an original combination of pavé-set diamonds and polished gold. Lucyk burnished the metal bordering the diamonds to a smooth finish

to contrast the small beads of gold between the gems. The synthesis of materials made a warm pool of twinkling light.

Peretti had sure aesthetic instincts. Born in Florence, she had a superb education in Switzerland and Rome, where she received a degree in interior design. As an independent young woman, she worked first for an architect in Italy, then as a successful model in Spain. From there she moved to New York in 1968. As a model and intimate friend of Giorgio di Sant' Angelo and Halston, she shared their philosophies. Soon she began to design jewelry that both clothes designers used to accessorize their collections. Her heart-shaped belt buckles and bud vase pendants became an instant success. Their sweeping organic shapes and smooth polished surfaces matched the style to perfection. Bloomingdale's, the New York department store, sold her pieces at Cul-de-Sac, a small accessories boutique for young designers. Following in the footsteps of Jean Schlumberger and David Webb, Peretti received the Coty Award in 1971.

Though Peretti's work was new and forward-looking, she loved Tiffany's past accomplishments and admired the firm's founder, Charles Lewis Tiffany, who had introduced the Tiffany diamond setting in the 1880s. She empathized with his desire to make diamonds available to a wide audience and she, too, applied herself to a single-stone diamond ring that could be worn as an engagement ring. Thinking of the modern woman on the go,

Opposite right: For the April 4, 1977, cover of *Newsweek,* a model photographed by Alberto Rizzo wore jewels by Elsa Peretti, "Diamonds by the Yard" and an "Open Heart" pendant. The feature article, "Jewelry's New Dazzle," began, "The 128.5-carat Tiffany diamond—and the smaller rocks in the cases around it—have long been the main attractions at the celebrated jewelry store on New York's Fifth Avenue. These days, however, the crowds head for tiny lopsided golden shaped earrings, silver and ivory cuff bracelets and minuscule diamonds dotted along delicate gold chains and sold 'by the yard' for necklaces. The landslide success of these unlikely pieces has sparked the most revolutionary changes in serious jewelry since the Renaissance. And oddly enough, it all began at staid old Tiffany's, with the arrival of a tempestuous Italian ex-model named Elsa Peretti."

At a 1974 Halston fashion show, Liza Minnelli wears the designer's bright pink Ultrasuede jacket and "Diamonds by the Yard," a wedding present from Peretti and Halston.

Opposite left: Elsa Peretti's first diamond jewel for Tiffany was "Diamonds by the Yard," a chain with twelve diamonds in different sizes set in collets mounted at uneven intervals. When asked by the *New York Times* (September 30, 1974) about the diamond jewel, Peretti responded, "It catches the light just like larger diamonds and it's not nearly so imposing." Two "Swan" diamond rings by Elsa Peretti (below right) feature a diamond in a bezel setting (a circle of gold that surrounds the gem at its girdle). The design got its name from the abstract swan's head at the terminals of the slender gold band.

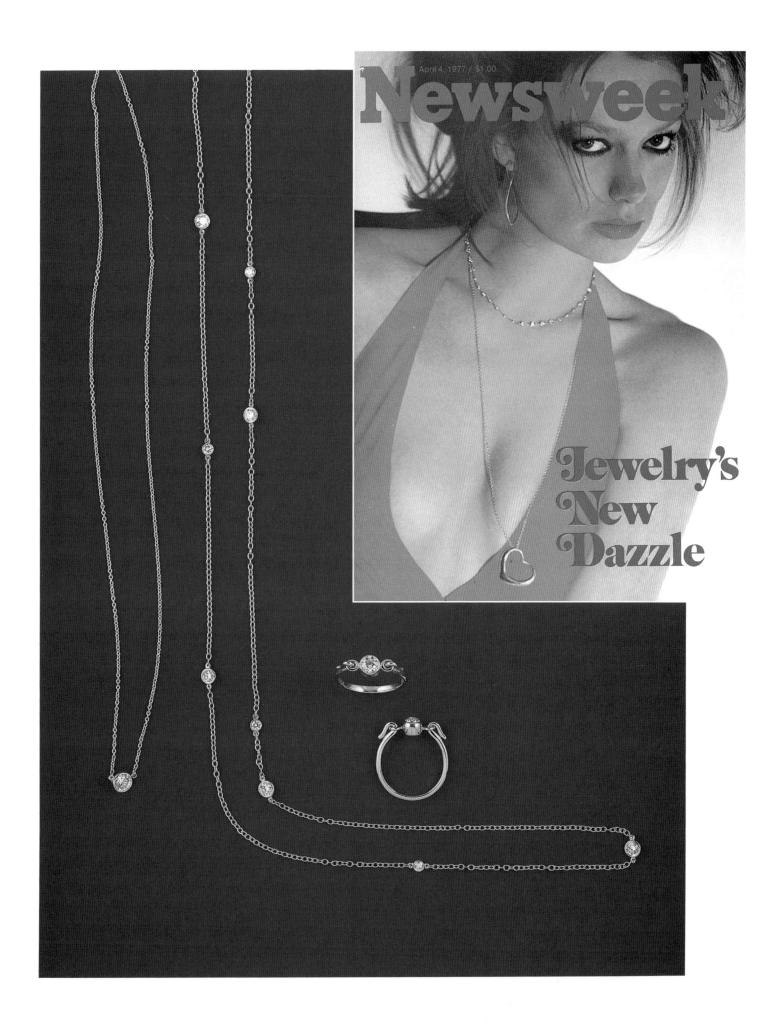

April 4, 1977 / $1.00

Newsweek

Jewelry's
New
Dazzle

she shied away from the classic prong setting, because of its potential for snagging on clothing and upholstery. Instead, she put the single diamond in a bezel setting, a strip of gold encircling the diamond at the girdle. This protected the diamond and presented no rough edges. A slender gold band terminating in two abstract swans heads held the bezel-set diamond in place. The "Swan" ring came in a range of carat weights from 0.23 to 0.89, hovering just below the much more expensive 1-carat diamond mark.

Peretti also loved the high end of Tiffany history, embodied by the Tiffany diamond. While her minimal style excluded making a wardrobe of settings for the Tiffany diamond, as Jean Schlumberger had done, she came up with a tribute to the 128.51-carat canary gem. In 1979, Peretti translated the shape and facets of the Tiffany diamond into an 18-karat-gold pendant, suspended from a twenty-six-inch black silk cord. Always thinking of the different sizes of her client's pocketbooks, she also made her Tiffany diamond in sterling silver. Peretti's "Tiffany Diamonds" were an original—and humorous—alternative to the big diamond look.

Well-made precious jewelry in the price range Elsa Peretti established for her line was so unprecedented that the 1977 *Newsweek* article on new jewelry designers proclaimed, "What Peretti had was a whole new idea of what jewelry should be. No longer serious, real jewelry has become accessible and affordable for every secretary and shopgirl." Explaining her approach to *New York Times* (September 30, 1974) fashion correspondent Bernadine Morris, Peretti said, "I make things that women like to touch and to wear, not things they put in a drawer."

Bulgari and Elsa Peretti transformed the image of the diamond in jewelry by creating pieces that worked with modern fashions and life-styles. Their success showed the importance of keeping up to date with fashion no matter how casual it became. Even though jewelers had always been concerned about staying current, they had not been forced to change their approach so radically since corsets gave way to the short skirts of the twenties, and formal lacy platinum and diamond styles gave way to geometric Art Deco forms. Bulgari and Elsa Peretti were the two jewelers working in the seventies who realized the urgency and necessity of change in order for diamonds to remain relevant to a woman's wardrobe. Elsa Peretti mentioned a woman's need for jewelry that she did not have to worry about and could wear disco dancing: "It was Studio 54 and you didn't want to lose anything" (*Mirabella*, December 1990). Bulgari called its pieces "Go-to-bed-with" jewels, meaning they could be worn around the clock and were so comfortable a woman might forget to take them off at night. These jewelers carved out a niche for designers who made pieces for women who had no desire for extravagant formal jewelry but still wanted a little genuine sparkle in their accessories.

Elsa Peretti's homage to Tiffany's history was a replica of the 128.51-carat
Tiffany diamond in gold suspended from a black silk cord. Peretti
extended the faceted-gold diamond look to other accessories, including
the "2 Carat" earrings. Even though one of Peretti's goals was to create
precious jewelry in a reasonable price range, she liked diamonds and
worked around the issue of cost by using small and sometimes
minuscule gems and transferring their faceted shapes into gold,
a less expensive alternative.

CHAPTER 10

PINK DIAMONDS

Up to the mid-eighties pink diamonds appeared only sporadically in jewelry. They had been almost as scarce as red, blue, and green diamonds, the three rarest colors, until the discovery of the Argyle mines in Australia. The new mines supplied enough volume to make pavé setting possible with pink diamonds, a milestone in jewelry. With the exception of canaries, colored diamonds had very little impact on jewelry trends, as the gems were simply unavailable. At the end of the twentieth century, pink diamond jewelry generated an excitement at auction reminiscent of that caused at the end of the nineteenth century by Empress Eugénie's crown jewels. The similarity extended to design. Pink diamonds inspired a contemporary take on the Versailles code of motifs, as well as fresh looks of a decidedly quirkier nature, from polka dots to bunnies.

The adventure of the pink diamond bonanza began in 1895, when a few diamonds were discovered "down under," suggesting to Australians that their country must have a deposit of them somewhere. It did, but not until a century later, in October 1979, was it located in the Kimberleys region of Western Australia. The AK1 Argyle diamond pipe (named after a nearby lake) and its riches have confounded the doubters and dazzled the experts. It is, without a doubt, the diamond success story of the late twentieth century, easily the foremost producer of diamonds in the world, and as if this were not enough, in 1984 Argyle became the first mine ever to produce a steady supply of fine small pink diamonds.

Basically, pink diamonds are pink due to atomic defects in the octahedral structure of the gem. Excluding Argyle, this accident of nature showed up sporadically in the famous diamond regions of India, Brazil, and South Africa. Only a few large pinks have been documented, and their progress through history reads like a who's who of merchants, explorers, and royalty. The 60-carat Nur-Ul-Ain (Light of the Eye) passed through the hands of gem merchant Jean-Baptiste Tavernier (purveyor to Louis XIV), Mogul emperors, and Persian conquerors before it was mounted in a tiara by Harry Winston for Shanbanou Farah of Iran. Ardent royalist John Williamson gave Queen Elizabeth II a pink diamond from his mine in Tanzania. The flawless 23.6-carat Williamson Pink, mounted in a white diamond daffodil Cartier

The pink diamond bow necklace by gem specialist and jeweler Ralph Esmerian features Australian pink diamonds and a 5.57-carat pear-shaped Brazilian pink diamond, mounted in platinum. The Esmerian jewel is credited with launching the craze for pink diamonds from the Argyle mines in Australia.

brooch, was seen on television by the world when the queen wore it during the 1981 wedding of Prince Charles and Lady Diana. In the United States, a country without pomp and circumstance, where the exhibition halls of museums replace the treasuries of potentates and royalty, Harry Winston introduced the 12.03-carat Martian Pink at the 1976 opening of the Gem and Mineral Hall of the American Museum of Natural History in New York. The diamond's name celebrated the successful landing of a scientific probe on Mars.

Leaving these mega "name" notables aside, most pink diamonds in the pre–Argyle mine era figured in jewelry as individual center stones. Their rarity and expense made each appearance a special occasion. After the discovery of the Argyle mines, small pink diamonds, the great majority ranging in size from 0.02 to 1 carat, became available in quantity and in a variety of shades: purplish cotton candy pink, raspberry pink, rosé wine pink, and seashell. Technically, pinks from Australia are distinguished from others by a unique combination of the following characteristics: frosted surface, birefringence (they split light into two unequally refracted waves), luminescence, and small colorless crystals. In addition, their minuscule pink grains are so close together that under a microscope they look like "brushstroke" graining, as artistically described by gemologist Stephen C. Hofer in his article "Pink Diamonds from Australia" in *Gems & Gemology* (Fall 1985).

The bad news about outback pinks is they come only in small sizes, usually less than half a carat. This is, in fact, a problem that plagues all Australian diamonds; because the rough is highly flawed, most of the stone must be cut away to produce a quality gem. But making up in quantity for what is lacking in size, jewelers and designers pavé set the gem and cluster it. They also channel set it in lines of pink gold and sink it into materials with dark contrasting colors. An overall uniform style has not emerged with pink diamonds; jewelers incorporate it into their own individual styles.

The first all-pink diamond jewel that appeared on the open market was a piece by the colored-gem specialist and jeweler Ralph Esmerian, a name that is synonymous with the most sophisticated designs and the highest quality gemstones. In 1890 Esmerian's grandfather Paul, a lapidary, moved from Constantinople to Paris, where he became a part of the elite coterie of Armenian gem dealers. His son Raphael joined the business in 1919 and helped make it the leading purveyor of precious gems in Europe, supplying the lion's share of colored stones to Cartier, among other firms. In 1939, with World War II on the horizon, Raphael Esmerian moved the business to New York City at the invitation of Raymond C. Yard. Esmerian's arrival in New York assured Yard and other leading American jewelers an access to stones of a quality formerly available only in Europe. Looking back on his position in the hierarchy of jewelry, Christie's auction house (*Magnificent Jewels*, New York, April 1995) called Esmerian "one of the most prominent gem dealers of all time." In 1976 Ralph Esmerian inherited his father's firm and carried on the tradition of creating and supplying magnificent jewelry and gem-quality stones to fine jewelers such as Cartier, Boucheron, Van Cleef & Arpels, and Tiffany & Co.

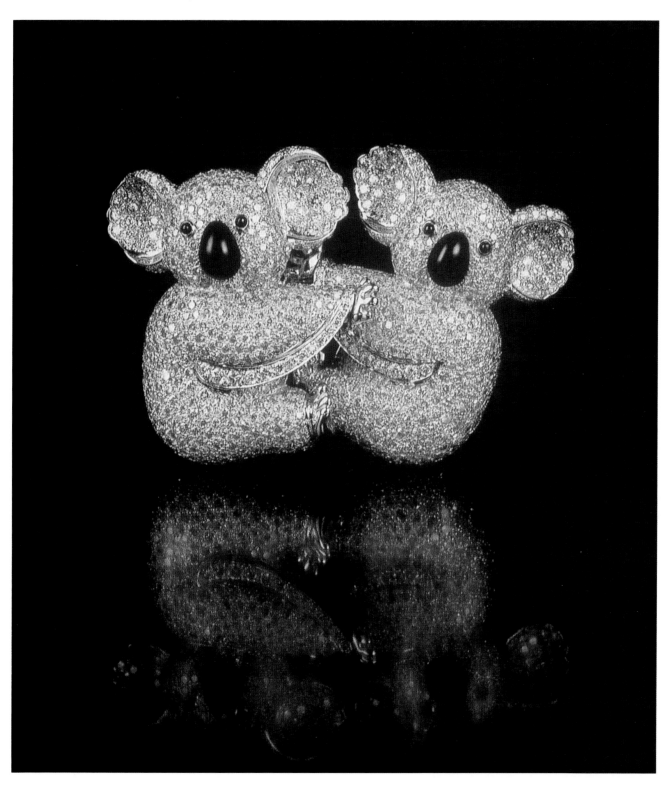

Koala bears appear in a brooch by Graff that displays pink diamonds set in pink gold, white diamonds set in white gold, and black onyx. The delightful jewel captures the spirit of Australia with the country's pink diamonds applied to its beloved marsupial.

When Esmerian first saw Australian pink diamonds, he described them as having "enormous charm." His bow necklace was the result of years spent gathering very fine examples of the gem. Then he obtained a Brazilian pink of 5.57 carats that was pure in color and fully saturated. According to Esmerian, the only way the magical South American could be mounted "so that its color would not be dwarfed by other gemstones" was to mount it with the Australian pinks. Describing the process, Esmerian explained, "A designer has ideas and makes sketches, then finds the gems. But a jeweler takes the opposite road. A jeweler buys stones and then realizes there is a jewel—it arises from the gemstones." The design of the pink diamond bow necklace was minimal in look, but it set off gemological fireworks. A line of circular-cut pink diamonds suspended a pear-shaped pendant with a delicate bow holding the Brazilian gem. All the gems were perfectly matched, an astonishing feat considering the highly flawed nature of Australian pinks.

Jewels like this one, once-in-a-lifetime pieces, revealed the key to the jeweler's art: the best of man and the best of nature. When the Esmerian bow necklace was sold by a private collector at Christie's-Geneva in May 1992, it attracted a cadre of elite and discreet jewelry buyers. François Curiel, Christie's International jewelry director, opened the bidding at $1 million. Seven hands immediately flew into the air and remained active up to $1.5 million. The jewel eventually sold for $1.8 million to a mysterious buyer. In order to remain anonymous, the buyer bid through a Swiss banker whose identity was also concealed, as he used a code name and had to be called in a hotel room instead of an office. "To this day," Curiel said, "we do not know who the collector was."

The first retail jeweler to embrace pink diamonds enthusiastically was Graff. Established in 1960 by Laurence Graff, the London jeweler has followed in the footsteps of Harry Winston. He is known worldwide for purchasing big diamonds and making megatransactions in high-carat-weight diamond jewelry. Some of the illustrious diamonds that have passed through Graff's hands include the Idol's Eye and the Porter Rhodes, a 54.99-carat diamond found at Kimberley in 1880. (Before Graff purchased the Porter Rhodes, it belonged to the Duke of Westminster and Harry Winston.)

Graff has combined pink diamonds with a magnificent array of colored diamonds in fancy cuts. For one bracelet, the jeweler assembled pear-shaped, marquise-cut, square, and circular-cut canary, blue, and other shades of colored diamonds with a handful of pink diamonds worked into a design like a jigsaw puzzle. Marquise-cut pink diamonds bordered the rainbow of gems. Among Graff's playful pink diamond jewels are butterfly and panther brooches. The jeweler saluted the Australian pink diamond discovery with a brooch depicting two pink diamond koala bears in an embrace.

Artist Daniel Brush said pink diamonds drove him to make something "heart-poundingly tender." Brush, celebrated for his technical virtuosity, conceives and fabricates his own jewelry. A former tenured fine arts professor at Georgetown University, Brush left the academic world to develop his expertise in ancient and modern techniques, specifically, granulation, steelwork,

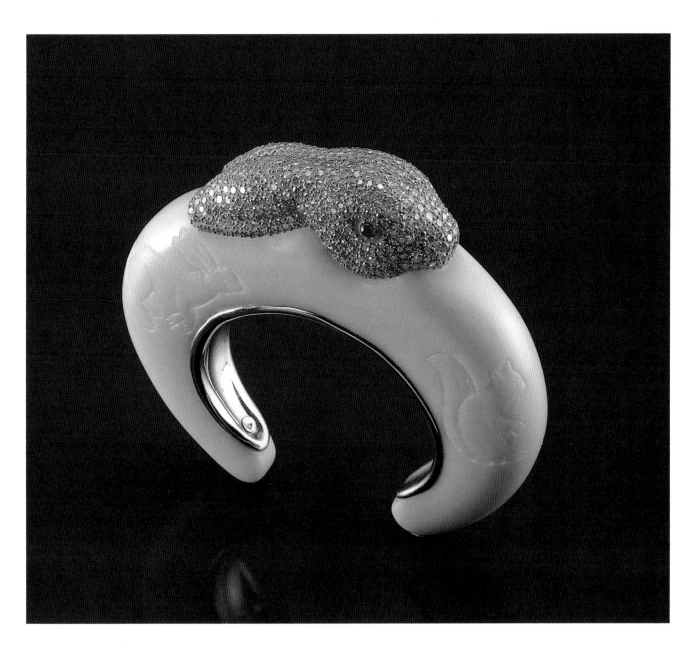

Playful in materials and design, the "Bunny Bangle" by Daniel Brush features the offbeat combination of pink diamonds mounted with pink gold prongs in Bakelite. Brush applied pink diamonds in subtle color gradations to accentuate the contours of the bunny head.

chiseling and inlaying steel with gold, and the eighteenth-century "art of turning" practiced on the original lathes. Brush also looks to the future by applying space-age solutions from the fields of aeronautical engineering and physics to metal objects. His archaeological pieces designed in the spirit of Etruscan gold work and his intimate hand-held steel and gold sculptures have been purchased by collectors who seek artistic precious objects and have an elevated appreciation for fine craftsmanship.

When Brush worked with pink diamonds, the first thing that popped into his mind was bunny rabbits. The inspiration for the form of Brush's pink diamond jewel—affectionately called "Bunny Bangle"—was a Chanel costume cuff, which he thought "kind of ugly." He wanted to improve it, so he took a single piece of forties pink Bakelite and modeled it into a cuff, carving the sides with rabbits and one squirrel and crowning the top with a bunny head. He set the piece ablaze with pink diamonds subtly graded by color to accentuate the shadows of the bunny's ears and head.

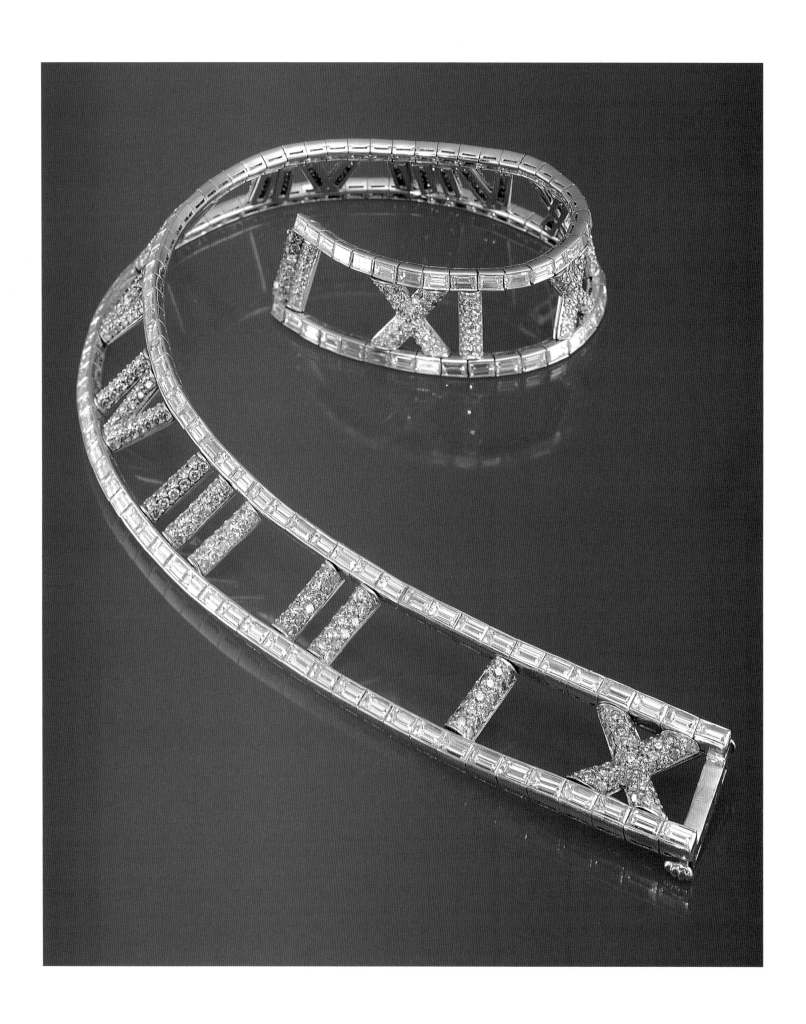

Opposite: The "Clock" necklace by Rachelle Epstein of Shelle combines pavé-set pink diamond Roman numerals with bands of baguette-cut white diamonds mounted in platinum. The sophisticated wit of transforming a clock face into a formal diamond necklace is characteristic of Epstein's work.

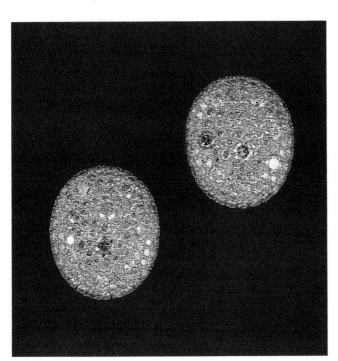

Rachelle Epstein combined pink and blue diamonds in a pair of polka dot button earrings, creating a colored diamond extravaganza.

With its pink diamonds sunk in industrial plastic, "Bunny Bangle" seemed to be totally irreverent on the surface, breaking down the division between costume and precious jewelry. Hidden in the piece's mischievous sweetness, however, were the intricate details of its creation. Brush had begun by hollowing out the Bakelite and piercing it with pink-gold prongs, using four or more to hold each pink diamond in place on the undulating planes. Low on the Mohs' scale of hardness, the Bakelite could have caved in at any moment during the fabrication. But, Brush emphasized, the manufacturing process was "merely speaking the language." The technical skill involved, he said, must bow to the overall concept, which should be—and certainly was in this case—"smile producing," with no hint of the intensive labor that went into it. Stanley Marcus, of Neiman-Marcus fame, called the bangle one of the "most delightful" objects he had ever seen.

Jewelry designer Rachelle Epstein of Shelle at Bergdorf Goodman playfully added pink diamonds to her spirited jewelry. Epstein's open attitude toward precious jewelry design stemmed from her education—she received a master's degree in painting from Yale—and experience as a costume jewelry designer. Her costume pieces revolved around found objects: rabbits' feet, dice, and other oddments. After viewing a private jewelry collection that included Lalique, Cartier, and Van Cleef & Arpels, Epstein switched to precious gems, explaining, "It was the same principle as oil paint to acrylic. The naturalness of the real material was overwhelming." When Epstein started designing precious jewelry, she increased the quality and value of her materials, and thus the cost. But she did not allow the higher stakes to influence her work. Epstein has continued to experiment and maintain a whimsical approach.

Her first pink diamond design was a gold bracelet made for daytime wear with the post-Argyle mantra "In the Pink" spelled out with pink diamonds. She took engraving, a feature usually hidden on the interior of a jewel, and boldly placed it on the exterior, further emphasizing the message by tracing it with pink diamonds. One of her most magnificent pieces conceived with the gem was the "Clock" necklace. Her initial inspiration for the piece was the portrait *Madame X* by John Singer Sargent. Pondering the painting, she suddenly realized the lady was only half-dressed without jewelry, and she designed the "Clock" necklace with Madame X in mind. The jewel incorporated two rows of baguette-cut diamonds enclosing Roman numerals, appropriated by Epstein from the face of a Cartier mystery clock. Adding another twist, Epstein defined the Roman numerals with pavé-set pink diamonds.

Even though the discovery of the Argyle mines made pink diamonds accessible, they still commanded a steep price. For pieces with a number of fine Australian diamonds or a multitude arranged in pavé settings, like the one-of-a-kind jewels by Ralph Esmerian, Graff, Daniel Brush, and

Long-stem pink diamond rose earrings designed by Christopher Walling and manufactured by Carvin French feature blossoms, buds, and stems of pink diamonds mounted in pink gold and leaves of olivine mounted in green gold (an alloy of gold with a varying percentage of silver, zinc, or cadmium). The pink on pink of Argyle diamonds and pink gold is a trend found in many pink diamond jewels, as the metal heightens the potency of the colored gems.

Rachelle Epstein, the prices escalated rapidly to tens of thousands and hundreds of thousands of dollars, because of the quality and quantity of gems, to say nothing of the original designs. In order to make their gem accessible to more people, Argyle Diamonds, the company representing the Argyle mines, commissioned jewelry designer Christopher Walling to come up with a line of pink diamond jewelry that could be worn just as easily with a business suit as an evening dress.

One of the reasons Argyle Diamonds selected Walling was because he had already demonstrated a flair with pink diamonds. He had designed a pair of quince earrings with pink diamonds set in pink gold blossoms, demantoid garnets in green gold leaves, and diamond and platinum stems. Another attraction for Argyle was that Walling had enjoyed success with jewels geared toward executive women, the firm's target audience. The X-shaped Biwa pearls worked into special settings for necklaces, bracelets, and earrings that composed his best-selling line showed that Walling could hone a signature look.

Walling chose Carvin French, one of the best manufacturing firms in the world, headed by André Chervin, to fabricate the quince earrings. With an expertise in virtually every aspect of hand craftsmanship, including platinum- and goldsmithing, precious stone cutting and engraving, and enameling, Carvin French has manufactured jewels for Tiffany, Van Cleef & Arpels, Bulgari, and Raymond C. Yard, as well as art jewelers such as Verdura and Schlumberger. Carvin French transformed the Walling design into three-dimensional, sculptural blooms. The extraordinary design and manufacture of the jewel conjured up both the Versailles code of motifs and thirties naturalism. When the earrings appeared at Christie's-New York special "American Jewelry" auction in 1992, credited "C. Walling—Carvin French," they exceeded the estimate of $50,000 to $60,000, climbing to a final hammer price of $104,500. Another impressive jewel by Walling and Carvin French was a pair of pink diamond long-stem rose earrings.

Walling's fascination with jewelry making and design began as a child. His father had learned jewelry technology at the Connecticut boarding school Avon Old Farms, and he taught his son metalworking. At age eight Walling received what amounted to a classical European apprenticeship, cutting the heads out of nickels, soldering, and working with a spirit lamp and blowpipe. Later on, Walling's close friend and mentor Suzanne Belperron inspired and encouraged him in the initial stages of his career to pursue his dream of becoming a jewelry designer. Walling has always maintained Belperron's artistic aesthetic of incorporating unusual materials into precious jewelry, and he shares her sense of solid color.

The Walling jewels from the Argyle Diamonds commission featured a minimal number of pink diamonds placed against dark fields of color for contrast. He channel set the pink diamonds in pink gold against oxidized silver and chose additional materials to provide drama—ebony and black Tahitian pearls, two dark, lustrous backgrounds that enhanced the gem and helped keep prices down. The most minimal jewels of the lot were ebony earrings inlaid with 0.6-carat diamonds set in pink gold. These jewels anchor the price of a pink diamond accessory to a few thousand dollars. The collection was named "Logic," because that describes the shape of the geometric forms and because the jewelry is a logical alternative to pink diamond jewels that carried extravagant price tags.

The less expensive pink diamond jewelry created by Walling offered pretty pink diamond designs to a larger audience. But the real jewelry breakthroughs and high-voltage thrills centered on designer pieces that daringly employed an abundance of pink diamonds with no bow to moderation. In 1995, when a second Esmerian pink diamond jewel—a bow brooch suspending a rare yellowish green diamond—appeared on the open auction market at Christie's in New York, it caused a sensation because of its design and unprecedented duet of colored diamonds.

Arguably, pink diamond jewelry opened people's eyes to the beauty of colored diamonds and created a connoisseurship for the gems. The desire to own the rarest varieties, especially blue ones, sent prices skyrocketing during the late eighties and nineties. Because these gems were for the most part sold individually and unmounted, a special excitement is unleashed when a jewel of extraordinary quality, like the Esmerian brooch, comes on the open market at auction. For the article "Now, the Color of Diamonds" in the *International Herald Tribune* (April 29–30, 1995), critic Souren Melikian explained, "The concern for rarity and personality that lies behind the rise of colored diamonds is typical of an art collector's attitude. It has led to another trend attached to design and signatures. Without it, the Esmerian brooch would

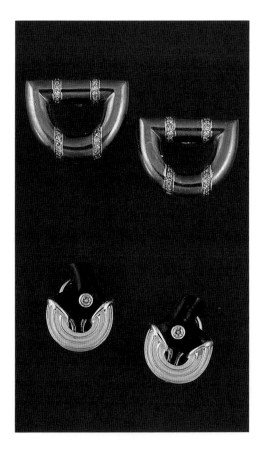

Two pairs of earrings from the "Logic" collection by Christopher Walling exploit the dramatic juxtaposition of pink diamonds set in pink gold against a dark substratum. The pair at the top has oxidized silver and the pair at the bottom includes ebony.

not have risen so high [$706,500]. The combination of green and pink is one of Esmerian's many inventions that he used to enhance designs rooted in the 18th-century tradition."

At the end of the twentieth century, just when people thought all the great diamond mines in the world had been mapped out with the advanced scientific means available to geologists, the riches of Argyle came to light. This optimistic find on the brink of the twenty-first century created heightened excitement around diamond jewelry by adding rare gems to magnificent designs. Though the surface mine reserves of AK1 are predicted to be exhausted by 2004, the Argyle mines raised the possibility that other diamond sources might be out there, a tantalizing prospect for designers. As Rachelle Epstein said in a moment of wishful thinking, "I hope I'm around when they discover the blue diamond equivalent of the Argyle mines."

The pink diamond bow brooch by Ralph Esmerian revives the shape of Empress Eugénie's white diamond bow by Kramer (see page 10). At the center knot, sixteen marquise-cut pink diamonds surround a 2.05-carat rhomboid-cut (a parallelogram with step cuts) pink diamond. A platinum mounting with a pink gold wash sets off the color of the gems.

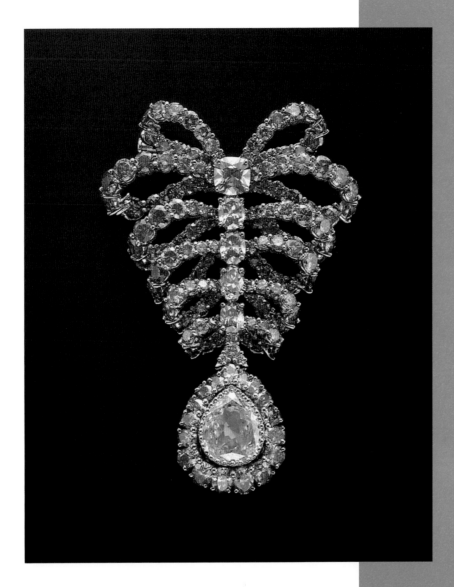

The form of the pink diamond brooch mounted in rose and
yellow gold by Ralph Esmerian came from an eighteenth-
century bow, but the addition of a 3.95-carat yellowish
green pear-shaped diamond to the all-pink diamond design
cast it in a new light. When this jewel was sold at auction
in 1995, it was placed on the cover of Christie's-New York
catalogue and admired for its graceful design, rare gems,
and original color scheme.

An exquisite diamond necklace mounted in platinum by Harry Winston features 10 large pear-shaped diamonds in graduated sizes from 5.12 to 19.79 carats, totaling 99.34 carats, 35 pear-shaped diamonds totaling 44.65 carats, 38 marquise-cut diamonds totaling 34.93 carats, and 85 round diamonds totaling 59.74 carats. The necklace shows the resiliency of Winston's holly wreath setting and its capacity to sustain enormous carat weights.

CHAPTER 11

DIAMOND JEWELRY IN THE NINETIES: A LOOK FORWARD AND BACK

When Barbra Streisand won the 1995 Emmy for her HBO concert special, she wore her multitier platinum and diamond necklace from around 1900 by Tiffany with a Donna Karan dress.

Throughout the twentieth century every period has had its own diamond jewelry style and, generally, every generation has regarded the one that came before it as passé. Art Deco rendered lacy platinum and diamond jewelry styles obsolete in the twenties; fifties all-diamond formalism replaced the gold styles of the forties; creative jewelry dislodged fifties formalism and then bowed to seventies minimalism. During the nineties, as the twentieth century draws to a close, almost all the diamond jewelry styles of the last hundred years—and some that are even older—exist simultaneously, and not one is considered dated or dowdy. Beauty alone is the criterion by which diamond jewelry is judged. A woman, whether star, socialite, model, or executive, chooses her jewelry to match her temperament, personality, and image. To suit the elegant atmosphere of her 1995 concerts, Barbra Streisand made her diamond and platinum Tiffany necklace from around 1900 a part of her stage attire. For Marla Maples's society column wedding to Donald Trump at the Plaza Hotel, the bride chose a Harry Winston tiara featuring pear-shaped and marquise-cut diamonds. In keeping with her sexy, supermodel image, Cindy Crawford wears, almost daily, a sporty single-stone version of Elsa Peretti's "Diamonds by the Yard."

The big jewelers that rose to prominence during the twentieth century, notably Bulgari, Cartier, Tiffany, Van Cleef & Arpels, and Harry Winston—nicknamed the Fifth Avenue jewelers because of their locations on the same street in New York City—have attained the stature of crown jewelers. Their names are the best known and the most distinguished. They deal in the biggest diamonds and they have all created diamond masterpieces for crowned heads and high-profile celebrities. To perpetuate their histories in the nineties, these jewelers play on the various themes in diamonds that have formed their images and made them famous.

The powerhouse of formal diamond jewelry styles of the twentieth century, Winston's signature all-diamond accessories—featuring good-size pear-shaped and marquise-cut diamonds with minimal platinum mountings—have been made so consistently over the last fifty years that they have become the epitome of formal diamond jewelry at the end of the century. In essence,

Above: For the 1994 CFDA (Council of Fashion Designers of America) Awards, rock star David Bowie escorts his wife, actress, model, and cosmetics magnate Iman, who wears a formal diamond necklace. Her jewel is reminiscent of the diamond styles of the 1950s that originated the lavish modern look of many diamonds clustered closely together.

Above right: At the 1993 Academy Awards, when Elizabeth Taylor received the Jean Hersholt Humanitarian Award for her crusade against AIDS, she wore her white and yellow diamond daisy necklace with chrysoprase leaves by Van Cleef & Arpels with her Valentino dress.

Donald Trump poses with his bride Marla Maples at their December 20, 1993, wedding at the Plaza Hotel in the Grand Ballroom. For the occasion, the bride got "something borrowed" from Winston—a $2 million diamond tiara to wear with her Carolina Herrera wedding dress. On her hand gleams a 7.45-carat diamond engagement ring, also from Winston. The Trumps' wedding involved jewelers up and down Fifth Avenue, including, in addition to Winston, Cartier and Tiffany, inasmuch as the couple registered at both places, and they named their daughter after the jewelry firm that allowed Trump to erect his tower in its air space.

Right: At the 1994 Academy Awards Sharon Stone dazzled onlookers when she made her entrance to the Dorothy Chandler Pavilion wearing the "Spirit of Beauty" brooch by Van Cleef & Arpels.

Far right: Cindy Crawford wears her Peretti "Diamonds by the Yard" with diamond stud earrings at the 1992 Beauty Ball Benefit for the March of Dimes.

For the 1995 Academy Awards, Stedman Graham escorts Oprah Winfrey, who wears diamond pendant earrings and a V-shaped diamond necklace suspending a pear-shaped diamond drop with a Gianfranco Ferré dress. The simple line of her necklace, made to show off a large stone, originated in the fifties, when formal diamond styles reached an all-time high in popularity.

Winston pieces are the most important source of inspiration for jewelers creating formal diamond looks.

The flower has been a leitmotiv of Van Cleef & Arpels since Alfred Van Cleef bought a floweret at the auction of the Diamonds of the Crown of France in 1887. In the 1990s the firm has updated the motif with flowers like the daisy set with two different colors of diamonds. Elizabeth Taylor showed off her white and canary diamond daisy collar with chrysoprase leaves by Van Cleef & Arpels at the 1993 Oscar ceremonies. The firm dips into its archives to bring back celebrated creations. For the fiftieth anniversary of the New York branch, it remade the all-diamond "Spirit of Beauty" brooch, a sprite with a wand and wings that exemplified the whimsy and grandeur of Van Cleef & Arpels. Sharon Stone wore the special piece at the 1994 Academy Awards ceremonies.

The panther has become Cartier's unofficial emblem. Toussaint's pack of cats have run off in all directions as the firm creates variations on the design. One of the new panther styles is a diamond bracelet with a three-dimensional panther head that lifts up to reveal a watch face. Even when the body of the beast is removed, its diamond hide spotted with gems is immediately recognizable. Large oval diamond and sapphire or onyx spotted hoop earrings form a bold variation on the panther theme.

Though its history is long and varied, Tiffany manages to balance all the various phases. The Tiffany Setting, made for solitaire diamonds in 1886, continues to be a popular choice for brides of the 1990s. Tiffany's byline designers create three very different images for the firm. Jean Schlumberger's designs, produced from his original ink and gouache drawings, offer bold, gemmy extravaganzas. Elsa Peretti's minimal diamond jewelry is as popular with the supermodels of the nineties as it was with the "Ultrasuaves" of the seventies. The work of Paloma Picasso, who started at Tiffany in 1980, is cherished by executive women with flair. Some of her signature designs include the "X" motif, the "XXXOOO" motif called "Love and Kisses," the "Loving Heart," and the "Scribble." These designs, transformed into earrings, brooches, and necklaces, are made in different versions: silver, gold, or gold studded with diamonds. For her fifteenth-anniversary celebration in 1995, Picasso revamped several of her designs. A jewel called "Little Secrets" summarized Picasso's design vocabulary: the large gold "X" brooch displayed miniature "Scribbles," "Xs," and "Loving Hearts" in diamonds set in platinum. William Chaney, chairman of the board of Tiffany, praised Picasso's contribution in *Town & Country* (November 1995), saying, "Her designs have exceeded all our expectations."

In 1989 Bulgari joined the big Fifth Avenue jewelers when it opened its largest branch in the world at Fifty-seventh Street and Fifth Avenue, across the street from Tiffany and Van Cleef & Arpels. Nicola Bulgari told *Women's Wear Daily* (November 3, 1989), "We will now have two design centers, here and in Rome." Always looking to the future, Bulgari continues to come up with breakthrough designs. One particularly creative jewel made in the mid-nineties was a thin collar necklace with the letters of the alphabet spelled out in diamonds. It made use of a new technology, the cutting of gems with a laser, a process that allows lapidaries to shape diamonds in any direction, forming figurative fashion gems, such as letters, ducks, horse heads, flowers, and stars. Bulgari has sustained its passion for the baguette-cut diamond, employing the shape in new and exciting ways, such as using tapered baguettes to fill out the curves of a hoop earring. Though other jewelers might be satisfied with two simple side stones for a diamond ring, Bulgari packs the

shank of its "Trombino" ring with baguettes acting as stepping-stones leading up to the rectangular diamond centerpiece. When asked about the firm's fondness for the diamond shape over the years, Nicola Bulgari exclaimed, "We flirt with the baguette."

The ideas of many twentieth-century jewelers who have passed away live on through their ink and gouache drawings, which provide a road map for the firms carrying on their names and legacies. Raymond C. Yard, a firm that has always had a discreet profile and a reputation for purveying the finest gems, continues to make beautiful diamond jewelry from the firm's archives as unobtrusively as ever. Robert Gibson, a son of one of Yard's partners, runs the firm, waiting patiently for the right stones to come his way so he can produce jewels from Yard design books that he knows by heart.

Verdura, Belperron, Seaman Schepps, and David Webb, jewelers who all used the diamond as a shiny accent against semiprecious materials and made unusual diamond pieces, have experienced a revival in the nineties.

A large gold "X" brooch by Paloma Picasso features three of her signature motifs, the "Loving Heart," the "Scribble," and the "X," in diamonds set in platinum. The jewel was named "Little Secrets," because the diamond motifs are indecipherable from a distance, but up close they reveal themselves.

Left: A diamond and gold "Trombino" ring by Bulgari features a "brick layer" of baguette-cut diamonds on the shank.

Opposite: The firm that carries on Verdura's name and legacy used one of his ink and gouache drawings to create the diamond lilac brooch mounted in platinum.

When the old designs of these jewelers are reproduced diamond for diamond, the jewelry looks just as contemporary as it did the first time around.

Edward Landrigan reestablished Verdura in 1985; the flair with which he has treated the duke's jewelry and image has made Verdura once again a favorite of the fashion press and jewelry lovers. Explaining what women of the nineties want to Stacey Okun for her *Town & Country* (June 1995) article, "The Two Gentlemen of Verdura," Landrigan said, "Today, women are looking for signature pieces, jewelry with soul. And that, above all, is Verdura's trademark." In 1991 Landrigan acquired the exclusive right to make the jewelry of Suzanne Belperron. This move put the work of two of the best and most innovative jewelers of the 1930s under one roof.

The jeweler who mixed diamonds with flea market finds at midcentury, Seaman Schepps has experienced a resurgence of popularity since the 1992 acquisition of the firm by Anthony Hopenhajm and Jay Bauer. Their inauguration party included a retrospective of the jeweler's work at the 485 Park Avenue Schepps salon. The event was followed by a catalogue illustrating a special collection of jewelry based on the work in the exhibition. The Schepps jewels caused a sensation in fashion magazines. *Vogue* (October 1992) reported, "Today, rediscovered molds and sketches by Schepps are the basis for designs newly available at the company's New York City store."

The son of David Webb's partner, Stanley Silberstein has continued the legacy of the firm. With its casual but dramatic effect, Webb jewelry is a favorite with nineties businesswomen who want accessories to carry them from daytime into evening. What was once the travel jewelry of the jet set is appropriate because of its minimal diamond look—spare enough for the office, but fancy enough for cocktail parties.

In 1993 Chanel reintroduced diamond jewelry to its repertoire of accessories. According to Barbara Cirkva, senior vice president, Fashion Division, Chanel, Inc., "The Chanel Joaillerie Collection includes faithful reproduc-

At the 1995 Emmy Awards, television star Christine Baranski wears the Chanel "Eternal Diamonds-Camellia" necklace with matching earrings, both with gold mountings, and a bustier gown also from Chanel. The jewel was not one of Chanel's original diamond designs of the 1930s, but its wraparound shape was inspired by some of the forms, and the flower is a motif closely identified with Chanel couture.

Opposite: The "Three Dove" brooch by Julius Cohen featuring one star-shaped diamond and white, pink, and canary diamonds mounted in gold and platinum was a family project. In March 1994, Leslie Steinweiss, Julius Cohen's son-in-law and head of the firm, traveled with his family and Julius Cohen to his nephew's wedding, where the canopy used to cover the wedding party at the Jewish ceremony was made by Steinweiss's parents, Alex and Blanche, an artist and weaver respectively. When Cohen saw the canopy he could not contain himself. He leaned over to Leslie Steinweiss during the ceremony and whispered, "That would make a helluva great-looking piece of jewelry." Back in New York they began working with jewelry designer-renderer Nina Giambelli on the jewel, which won a 1994 Diamonds Award.

The diamond ring Hillary Rodham Clinton wore to the 1992 presidential inauguration was designed by Henry Dunay around the Kahn canary diamond, a 4.23-carat natural (uncut) canary diamond from Crater of Diamonds, a state park in Murfreesboro, Arkansas. Dunay's setting symbolized the "Natural State," with platinum representing the clouds, green gold conjuring up the trees, and pavé-set diamonds alluding to the Arkansas lakes and streams. The Kahn canary diamond had a history for the First Family. Rodham Clinton wore it on two other inaugural occasions, when Bill Clinton took office as governor of Arkansas. At the 1986 National Governor's Conference Diamond Dinner, Bill Clinton exhibited the diamond, owned by jeweler Stanley Kahn of Pine Bluff, Arkansas, to publicize the uniqueness of the state's natural resources.

tions of some of Mademoiselle Chanel's personal favorites, as well as pieces inspired by her original designs but adapted to the women of the nineties." Since the diamond was Chanel's favorite gem, the focus of the collection is a group of diamond jewels, reeditions of her old designs, that include the "Fountain" and "Comet" necklaces, the "Fringe" bracelet, and the "Starburst" brooch. At the 1995 Emmy Awards, television actress Christine Baranski glittered in one of the best of the new designs, the wraparound necklace with a large camellia in diamonds and gold dubbed "Eternal Diamonds-Camellia."

The Diamonds Awards—Diamonds-International and Diamonds Today (formerly Diamonds USA)—have maintained their stance of rewarding cutting-edge designs and bringing jewelers to a large audience. Frequently, the winners are presented in touring exhibitions in art galleries around the country and honored with a special portfolio of images shot by art and fashion photographers. For the 1995 award winners, J. Walter Thompson, the advertising firm representing De Beers in New York and worldwide, invited Patrick Demarchelier—called by *Harper's Bazaar* (November 1995) "perhaps the most sought-after shooter of the '90s"—to photograph the jewels on models in his simple but glamorous style.

Certainly the jeweler who has participated in more Diamonds Awards competitions than any other is Julius Cohen Jeweler. The firm maintains a link with the Diamonds Awards of the past, going back to the early years when the awards were established in the postwar period, by consistently submitting and winning the honor. For the 1994 Diamonds Awards, Julius Cohen Jeweler kept up its long winning streak with the stunning "Three Dove" brooch, composed of white, pink, and canary diamonds mounted in gold and platinum. Leslie Steinweiss, Cohen's son-in-law, who took over the firm after Julius Cohen passed away in 1995, enjoys reviving Diamonds Award–winning designs from the past. A 1958 Diamonds Award winner that was completely ahead of its time, the "Flash and Roll" necklace of twirling cylindrical motifs flashing three different colors of diamonds inspired a modern rendition. Both designs featured white, canary, and cognac (a light brown shade named after the brandy) diamonds, but the contemporary version showed diamonds of more intense shades, reflecting the popularity of colored diamonds in the nineties.

One of the most consistent Diamonds Award winners over the last three decades, Henry Dunay won his first Diamonds-International Award in 1967. While Dunay found his inspiration in the natural world, his jewels do not resemble any naturalistic jewels of the past. He veers away from representational imagery in favor of what he likes to call "New Age" designs. According to Dunay, "Through my designs, I relate meaningful messages about the destiny of humankind. We must do all that we can to create and sustain an environment where we can harmoniously co-exist with our sphere." Free-form shapes of many different colors of gold, platinum, and silver combined with canary and white pavé-set diamonds are the hallmark of his multidimensional work. For the 1992 presidential inauguration, First Lady Hillary Rodham Clinton wore a Dunay ring. Inspired by the topography of Arkansas, the free-flowing design centered on the 4.23-carat natural

Opposite right: President Bill Clinton dances with First Lady Hillary Rodham Clinton at the 1992 Inaugural Ball. On her finger Rodham Clinton wears the Kahn canary diamond mounted in a free-form Henry Dunay ring.

(uncut) Kahn canary diamond, a gem found at Crater of Diamonds, a state park in Murfreesboro, Arkansas, where anybody can play prospector.

Among all the Diamonds Award winners, M + J Savitt stands out for introducing new places to wear diamond jewelry. Janis Savitt's interest in cutting-edge casual began during her high school years in the seventies, when Elsa Peretti transformed the image of diamond jewelry. Savitt recalled, "Before Elsa Peretti came around, there was nothing in terms of newness. By newness, I mean simplicity of form." With her two sisters, Michelle and Wynne, Janis Savitt established the firm M + J Savitt and has designed and purveyed jewelry in platinum, silver, and gold with minimal diamond accents—a woman's everyday jewels, pieces meant to be worn all the time. Following in the footsteps of Peretti, M + J Savitt won a Coty Award in 1984, the last time the award was given. In the nineties, Savitt has pushed the limits of places to wear diamond jewelry, igniting a widespread trend with dia-

Irving Penn photographed supermodel Christy Turlington wearing a navel ring with a cushion-shaped canary diamond by M + J Savitt for a *Vogue* (April 1994) feature about body piercing.

mond navel rings, pavé-set diamond nose rings, and waist chains with diamond charms. Though they may seem outlandish, unrealistic, or far-fetched on the surface, the nose and navel styles appear no more extreme to their adherents than the idea of wearing tiaras to dinner parties—a trend of the fifties that looks bizarre from a nineties perspective. Many supermodels wear diamond navel rings. Naomi Campbell had Tiffany extend the chain of her "Diamonds by the Yard" so she could wear it looped around her waist and through her navel ring. Pop icon Madonna has a diamond horseshoe charm attached to her navel ring and sports a diamond stud in her nose.

As the nineties has been touted the decade of quality rather than quantity, many fashion designers who might have been making costume jewelry in

Too tiny to be worn on the finger, Isaac Mizrahi's "Angel Rings" are collected on a slender platinum chain as symbols of love or friendship. The miniature platinum rings show diamonds in prong settings and set around a wide band. Lazare Kaplan International cut the diamonds specially for Mizrahi, putting microscopic signatures, Mizrahi and Lazare Kaplan, at the outer perimeter of the gems.

another era have joined the ranks of precious jewelry designers. Fashion notables who have won recognition for their jewelry include American designers Isaac Mizrahi and Marc Jacobs and Italian designer Gianni Versace. The gem of choice among all three is the diamond. Versace has created a collection of rings with diamond borders enclosing the Medusa emblem of his couture house. The former designer for Perry Ellis, Marc Jacobs, famous for launching the "grunge" look in 1992—based on flannel shirts and thrift shop finds—inspired by Seattle rock, reversed his style when he started designing glamorous clothes and diamond jewelry under his own name. His jewelry included pavé-set diamond disk and numeral earrings. Mizrahi dreamed up "Angel Rings," a play on the old high school custom of a girl wearing her boyfriend's ring on a chain. Mizrahi's version, however, was infinitely more sophisticated. Several miniature prong-set platinum and diamond engagement rings and a diamond-set wide band hang from a thin platinum chain. The gems were created specially for the Mizrahi jewel by one of the oldest and most celebrated

American lapidaries, Lazare Kaplan. Established in 1903, the firm is best known for cutting the 726-carat Jonker diamond in 1934.

Old diamond shapes, especially rose cuts, that originated hundreds of years ago and lack the brightness of twentieth-century shapes have been reassessed in the nineties. Explaining why his family firm likes old shapes, Mario Buccellati said, "You don't always want a blinding surface of light." The popularity of old diamond shapes that had been considered inferior throughout the twentieth century has been so overwhelming that lapidaries are producing them again, especially rose cuts.

Some jewelers have revived the materials applied historically to diamond decorations. Silver, the metal that all but disappeared with the switch

The pavé-set diamond and platinum dragonfly brooch by Fred Leighton features baguette-cut diamonds at two cross points on the body and bulging ruby eyes. Turn-of-the-century insect jewelry inspired the design, but Leighton's version is much larger than its antique predecessors. In addition, the closely packed circular-cut diamonds, covering the articulated tail and divided into segments by openwork veins on the wings, give the piece a distinctly modern look.

Ex-wife of Metromedia mogul John Kluge, Patricia Kluge wears a canary diamond dragonfly brooch by Fred Leighton.

to platinum at the turn of the century, has made a comeback and is used by a number of jewelers with very different styles, from Henry Dunay to Christopher Walling to Buccellati to JAR. The black oxidization of a silver setting provides deep color and high contrast to the white light of the diamond. It is also an excellent background for pink diamonds.

Designs from the late nineteenth and early twentieth century have proved an inspiration for jewelers. They know their diamond jewelry history and are savvy about what they choose to apply to their work. From firsthand experience, Fred Leighton understands the ins-and-outs of antique jewelry like few others. An estate jeweler with a boutique on upper Madison Avenue in New York, Leighton became a major player in the creation of the estate jewelry market during the eighties, generating an enthusiasm and appreciation for the intricacies and beauty of period pieces. In the nineties he has augmented the antique jewelry in his boutique with clever modern renditions of some of the best diamond styles of the twentieth century. Leighton's contemporary jewels are not slavish imitations; he alters the proportions and changes the gems, outlines, and forms, coming up with accessories that display antique motifs but look completely contemporary in execution. One of his finest improvisations was inspired by turn-of-the-century gem-set dragonfly brooches. Leighton's huge diamond dragonfly brooch flaunts an articulated tail and a wingspan measuring a little over six inches.

An American designer working in Paris, Joel Arthur Rosenthal (whose initials form the name of his firm JAR) uses antique jewelry, especially eighteenth-century designs, as a source of inspiration. Working with his Swiss partner Pierre Jeannet in a discreet, almost hidden boutique in a walkway at 7 Place Vendôme, Rosenthal conceives pieces that could be mistaken for their period prototypes were it not for some imaginative twist. An eighteenth-century ring design with a heart-shaped motif served as the jumping-off point for a piquant Rosenthal jewel. He made the standard antique form his own by arranging old mine-cut greenish diamonds, extracted from an eighteenth-century watch, in the shape of a heart enclosing an oval-cut pink diamond; the ring's hoop displayed old mine-cut near-colorless diamonds. Spreading different shades of diamonds in old cuts across the surface of a single jewel makes for a nubby, woven tapestry-like effect that is characteristic of JAR jewelry. Rosenthal held down the different colors and textures of diamonds in the ring with an oxidized silver setting—a trademark of the firm. Rosenthal exploits the softness of silver to execute extraordinary pavé work with the gems tightly mounted together, achieving a remarkably striking and fresh overall effect. In JAR jewels details of antique designs become a fanciful play on jewelry history. For one series, Rosenthal grooved and twisted blackened silver into ribbon jewels whose inner folds were pavé set with diamonds. The clever designs immediately conjure up the craze for neck velvets and grosgrain ribbons at the turn of the century.

At the other end of the spectrum, jewelers of the 1990s have also turned to materials related to their time. The advent of the space-age metal titanium into diamond design has allowed jewelers to make oversize pieces almost as light as air, compatible with contemporary lightweight fabrics. Emmanuel Guillaume, who runs the Belgian jewelry firm ESG, has done extensive research with alloy specialists to develop titanium alloys. The metal is applied to the firm's nature-theme jewels designed by Guillaume's wife, Sophie. The properties of titanium allow Sophie Guillaume's imagination to take flight and express itself in lines that are more fluid than any nature-theme jewels of the past. Just as the natural world boasts a host of shades and gradations of color, so do ESG's jewels. These schemes, however, are not nature's coloration, they are Sophie's choice—whimsically recreated with the highest quality colored diamonds from around the world. Emmanuel Guillaume obtains fully saturated canary orange diamonds from Zaire and gray diamonds from South Africa and Brazil, among other shades. These mixes of colored diamonds in titanium settings result in exuberant and joyous modern jewelry. Though it is extremely difficult to work, titanium makes settings lighter and more resilient than platinum, gold, or silver. Under Guillaume's guidance the metal has become a promising material for jewelry in the twenty-first century.

From 1887 to 1995 jewelers have conceived a wider variety of diamond jewelry styles than in any other age. By mixing the old and new, jewelers of the nineties bear witness to Marshall McLuhan's theory that we look toward the future through a rearview mirror. What will the twenty-first century hold for diamond jewelry? If the approach of the nineties jewelers is any indication, diamond jewelry will become even more interesting and sophisticated.

Eighteenth-century jewelry inspired a ring by JAR with old mine-cut greenish diamonds (some backed with green enamel) centering on an oval-cut pink diamond. Old mine-cut near-colorless diamonds studding the hoop provide a subtle shift in color from the greenish diamonds decorating the heart-shaped motif. The gems are mounted in oxidized silver and gold prongs hold the pink diamond in place.

Blackened and grooved silver imitates grosgrain ribbon in a pair of earrings by JAR. Pavé-set diamonds line the reverse side of the ribbons, adding sparkle to the matte texture.

Butterfly earrings by ESG feature a
mixed-metal alloy consisting primarily
of titanium. The setting is so light that
each earring weighs only four grams.
A quartet of diamonds gives the butterflies
their patterning. Orange canary diamonds
(a fully saturated canary with a touch
of orange) fill out the wings, trimmed with
steel gray diamonds that shade the color
and finish off the edges. Bright white
diamonds make up the bodies. Canary
diamonds on the tips of the antennae
are contrasted with tiny white diamonds
set in iron. Hidden on the reverse are
heart-shaped ear pads pavé set with
white diamonds.

APPENDIX: JEWELERS' GALLERY

Frédéric Boucheron, in an 1895 portrait by Aimé Morot, distinguished himself at the sale of the Diamonds of the Crown of France by obtaining the Grand Mazarin. Boucheron was an innovator both in design and technology who also produced extravagant formal diamond pieces in the Versailles code for the likes of Spanish dancer La Belle Otéro and the American family of silver king John W. Mackay.

Charles Lewis Tiffany was called "the King of Diamonds" in the 1890s not only for his coup at the sale of the Diamonds of the Crown of France—he brought back to American over one-third of the collection— but also for the small diamond pieces and the Tiffany setting that put diamond jewelry within the reach of a broader audience.

A watercolor by René Binet of René Lalique, designing at his worktable, shows some of the jeweler's sources of inspiration as well as his own jewelry and models.

An 1895 photograph shows Henri Vever painting. Like so many of the Art Nouveau jewelers, Vever participated broadly in the arts. He enjoyed painting and design; he assembled a world-class collection of Islamic art, and he wrote extensively on jewelry history. His most famous book was a chronicle of French jewelers and manufacturers, the definitive *La Bijouterie française au XIXe siècle*.

On a 1911 trip to Bahrain to buy pearls, Jacques Cartier, one of the three Cartier brothers, took a moment to relax with some sheiks. The personal touch that the Cartier family brought to every aspect of its business in the early years of the century came through in its magnificent jewelry and made it one of the most successful firms of the era.

On his first trip to Russia in 1904, Pierre Cartier made his calls in a horse-drawn sleigh.

Louis Cartier, an avid yachtsman, sets sail with his dog. The most influential member of the Cartier family, Louis did not travel to exotic places as regularly as his brothers. Instead, he stayed in Paris and steered the creative course of the family firm.

A photograph shows Raymond C. Yard when he began his firm in the early twenties. The high quality of Yard's jewelry and the integrity of his business attracted American clients who might otherwise have shopped in Europe for their Art Deco jewelry. In addition to being one of the best American Art Deco jewelers, Yard was an amateur boxer and golfer.

Paul Flato as he appeared during his heyday in the mid-thirties. A name familiar to movie audiences, Flato jewelry could be seen frequently on the silver screen.

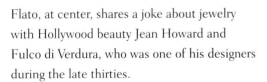

Flato, at center, shares a joke about jewelry with Hollywood beauty Jean Howard and Fulco di Verdura, who was one of his designers during the late thirties.

A 1931 photograph shows Jeanne Boivin sitting at her desk at the Boivin salon on the Avenue de l'Opéra. René Boivin's wife, Jeanne ran the firm from 1917, the year her husband died, to 1954 when she retired at the age of eighty-four.

Suzanne Belperron wears a jewel of her own design while sitting at her desk at B. Herz. Her partnership with Bernard Herz, a fruitful relationship, began in 1933; he manufactured the jewels she designed. The firm's successful run was interrupted by the onset of World War II. Herz, fearing the Nazis, put the enterprise into Belperron's name. During the war she had offers to leave occupied Paris, but she held on to the company tenaciously and was able to present it intact to Jean Herz after his father's death in a concentration camp. From 1945 to 1975 they ran Herz-Belperron together.

Fulco di Verdura's worldly sophistication is captured in a photograph by his friend Horst. After the jewelry designer left Flato and established his own firm at 712 Fifth Avenue in 1939, he became one of the foremost artistic jewelers.

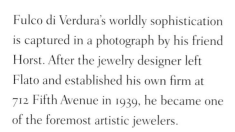

In the forties, Claude, Julien, and Louis Arpels, the three members of the Arpels family who ran Van Cleef & Arpels, posed for a picture in their New York salon, a replication of the Paris headquarters in miniature.

Life (March 17, 1952) illustrated an article on Harry Winston with a photograph of the jeweler hidden in the shadows of his Louis XV–style office at Rockefeller Center opposite Saint Patrick's Cathedral in New York. Because of the $10 million value of his Court of Jewels collection, Winston's insurance company did not want his face to be photographed and seen by potential jewelry thieves.

Tiffany's first byline designer, Jean Schlumberger posed for a photograph by Cecil Beaton in 1956.

When creative jewelry was at its peak in the mid-fifties and sixties, Parisian jeweler Pierre Sterlé rode the crest of the wave, designing all-diamond jewelry as well as an original series of bird brooches.

Julius Cohen holds his 1957 Diamonds-International Award. A multiple Diamonds Award winner, Cohen was unique among his contemporaries in his consistent use of large—20 carats and up—canary diamonds.

A member of the Diamonds-International Academy, New York jeweler Seaman Schepps won awards for diamond pieces that pushed the limits with unusual materials.

Cartier-Paris artistic director Jeanne Toussaint was photographed wearing a strawberry brooch and multiple strands of pearls. Although Cartier never featured byline designers for precious jewelry, Toussaint received media attention throughout the sixties as one of the most influential people behind the Cartier style. Toussaint had been with the firm since the teens, but her contributions gained recognition during this period when jewelry was not dominated by a uniform style, such as Art Deco, but instead defined by personal design choices.

Nicola, Gianni, and Paolo Bulgari (from left to right) transformed the family firm into an international enterprise and changed the perception of diamond jewelry during the 1970s. Their chic diamond jewels covered with baguettes and their gold chains enhanced with intaglios, coins, and diamonds were worn by women from daytime into evening.

Elsa Peretti became Tiffany's second byline designer in 1974. The "Flask" on a chain around her neck displays the sleek style that characterized her work.

Ralph Esmerian has done innovative work with pink Argyle diamonds that have ignited the market. As a counterpoint to his work in fine jewelry, Esmerian collects American folk art and is the president of the Museum of American Folk Art. Arnold Newman photographed Esmerian among his collection for the *Town & Country* article "Folk Art's Old Guard" (January 1990).

The London jeweler Laurence Graff, who established his firm Graff in 1960, has been called by many the Harry Winston of the eighties and nineties. He has handled many of the world's most famous "name" diamonds and has added significantly to the legacy of formal diamond jewelry with beautiful pink diamond pieces as well as other diamond jewels with rare colored gems.

Paloma Picasso, a byline designer at Tiffany since 1980, poses for a photograph wearing her pearl necklace that features gold segments studded with diamonds.

Joel Arthur Rosenthal was photographed in Paris where his firm JAR'S is located. Celebrated for his inspired improvisations on antique diamond jewelry, Rosenthal is one of the foremost designers of the nineties.

SELECTED BIBLIOGRAPHY

The Age of the Baroque in Portugal. Exhibition catalogue. Washington, D.C.: National Gallery of Art, 1994.

The Art of Cartier. Exhibition catalogue. Paris: Musée du Petit Palais, 1990.

Ash, Russell. *Sir Edward Burne-Jones.* New York: Harry N. Abrams, 1993.

Auchincloss, Louis. *The Vanderbilt Era: Profiles of a Gilded Age.* New York: Macmillan, 1989.

Balfour, Ian. *Famous Diamonds.* 2d ed. Colchester, Essex: N.A.G. Press, 1992.

Barten, Sigrid. *René Lalique: Schmuck und Objets d'art, 1890–1910.* Munich: Prestel-Verlag, 1977.

Becker, Vivienne. *Art Nouveau Jewelry.* New York: E. P. Dutton, 1985.

The Belle Epoque of French Jewellery, 1850–1910. Exhibition catalogue. Munich: Bayerisches Nationalmuseum, 1990.

Broido, Lucy. *The Posters of Jules Chéret.* New York: Dover Publications, 1980.

Bury, Shirley. *Jewellery, 1789–1910.* 2 vols. Suffolk: Antique Collectors' Club, 1991.

Cailles, Françoise. *René Boivin, Jeweller.* London: Quartet Books, 1994.

Cologni, Franco, and Eric Nussbaum. *Platinum by Cartier.* Translated by Lory Frankel. New York: Harry N. Abrams, 1996.

Elsa Peretti: Fifteen of My Fifty with Tiffany. Exhibition catalogue. New York: Fashion Institute of Technology, 1990.

Evans, Joan. *A History of Jewellery, 1100–1870.* London: Faber and Faber, 1953.

Ferguson, George. *Signs and Symbols in Christian Art.* New York: Oxford University Press, 1954.

Field, Leslie. *The Queen's Jewels: The Personal Collection of Elizabeth II.* New York: Harry N. Abrams, 1987.

Die Fouquet, 1860–1960, Schmuck-Künstler in Paris. Exhibition catalogue. Zurich: Museum Bellerive, 1984.

Gere, Charlotte, and John Culme with William Summers. *Garrard: The Crown Jewellers for 150 Years.* London: Quartet Books, 1993.

Le Grand Negoce. Organe du Commerce de Luxe Français. L'Exposition des Arts Décoratifs. Exhibition catalogue. Paris: La Société Anonyme de l'Imprimerie de Vaugirard, 1926.

Heskett, John. *Industrial Design.* London: Thames and Hudson, 1980.

Higgins, Reynold. *Greek and Roman Jewellery.* 2d ed. Berkeley and Los Angeles: University of California Press, 1980.

Howard, Jean. *Travels with Cole Porter.* New York: Harry N. Abrams, 1991.

A Jeweler's Eye: Islamic Arts of the Book from the Vever Collection. Exhibition catalogue. Washington, D. C.: Arthur M. Sackler Gallery, Smithsonian Institution, 1988.

Johnson, Paul. *Modern Times: The World from the Twenties to the Nineties.* Rev. ed. New York: HarperCollins, 1991.

Kanfer, Stefan. *The Last Empire: De Beers, Diamonds, and the World.* New York: Farrar Straus & Giroux, 1993.

Katz, Ephraim. *The Film Encyclopedia.* New York: Harper & Row, 1979.

Krashes, Laurence S. *Harry Winston: The Ultimate Jeweler.* Santa Monica: Gemological Institute of America, 1984.

Liddicoat, Richard T., ed. *The GIA Diamond Dictionary.* 3d ed. Santa Monica: Gemological Institute of America, 1993.

Morel, Bernard. *The French Crown Jewels.* Antwerp: Fonds Mercator, 1988.

Nadelhoffer, Hans. *Cartier: Jewelers Extraordinary.* New York: Harry N. Abrams, 1984.

Néret, Gilles. *Boucheron: Four Generations of a World-Renowned Jeweler.* New York: Rizzoli, 1988.

Newman, Harold. *An Illustrated Dictionary of Jewelry.* London: Thames and Hudson, 1981.

Pliny the Elder, Natural History: A Selection. Edited by John F. Healy, New York: Penguin Books, 1991.

Pojarskaïa, Militsa, and Tatiana Volodina. *L'Art des Ballets Russes, 1908–1929.* Paris: Gallimard, 1990.

Proddow, Penny, and Debra Healy. *American Jewelry: Glamour and Tradition.* New York: Rizzoli, 1987.

Proddow, Penny, Debra Healy, and Marion Fasel. *Hollywood Jewels: Movies, Jewelry, Stars.* New York: Harry N. Abrams, 1992.

Purtell, Joseph. *The Tiffany Touch.* New York: Random House, 1971.

Raulet, Sylvie. *Art Deco Jewelry.* New York: Rizzoli, 1985.
———. *Van Cleef & Arpels.* New York: Rizzoli, 1987.

Reade, Brian. *Art Nouveau and Alphonse Mucha.* London: Her Majesty's Stationery Office, 1963.

René Lalique. Exhibition catalogue. Paris: Musée des Arts Décoratifs, 1992.

Scarisbrick, Diana. *Rings: Symbols of Wealth, Power and Affection.* New York: Harry N. Abrams, 1993.

Schneirla, Peter, and Penny Proddow. *Tiffany: 150 Years of Gems and Jewelry.* Exhibition catalogue. New York: Tiffany & Co., 1987.

Snowman, A. Kenneth, ed. *The Master Jewelers.* New York: Harry N. Abrams, 1990.

A Sparkling Age: 17th-Century Diamond Jewellery. Exhibition catalogue. Antwerp: Diamond Museum, 1993.

Sutherland, Beth Benton. *The Romance of Seals and Engraved Gems.* New York: Macmillan, 1965.

Tolansky, S. *The History and Use of Diamond.* London: Shenval Press, 1962.

Vever, Henri. *Histoire de la Bijouterie Française au XIXe Siècle.* 3 vols. Paris: Imprimerie Georges Petit, 1908.

Zapata, Janet. *The Jewelry and Enamels of Louis Comfort Tiffany.* New York: Harry N. Abrams, 1993.

Zucker, Benjamin. *Gems and Jewels: A Connoisseur's Guide.* New York: Thames and Hudson, 1984.

ACKNOWLEDGMENTS

A cast of thousands helped us assemble the material for *Diamonds*. Many were there for the long haul, from start to finish; others came to our aid in specific areas. Everyone demonstrated extraordinary goodwill and we thank you all.

First and foremost we would like to single out Ralph Esmerian, whose insight and passion for jewelry have been a fount of inspiration for us as historians.

The following jewelers and families of jewelers have generously opened their archives and provided or helped us locate beautiful examples of diamond jewelry, giving sparkle to the modern history of the gem: Michel Bapst, heir to the jewelers of the crown of France; Buzz Baumgold; Alain Boucheron and Michel Tonnelot of Boucheron; Agnès Boudier-Sterlé; Daniel Brush; Mario Buccellati; Nicola Bulgari, Veronica Bulgari, and Catherine Robert of Bulgari; Eric Nussbaum, director of the Cartier Collection, Geneva; Bonnie Selfe, Ralph Destino, and Anne Holbach, archivist, of Cartier, New York; Maryam Saghatelian of Cartier, Beverly Hills; André Chervin of Carvin French; Gordon Roberts, executive director, and Amy Hoadley, public relations, of Chanel Joaillerie; Leslie Steinweiss, Bozidar Dordevic, and Joan Weiland of Julius Cohen Jeweler; Collingwood; Henry Dunay; Paul Flato and his daughters Catharine Dennis, Barbara McCluer, and Susie Flato; David V. Thomas and Corinna Pike of Garrard; Gwendoline Keywood of Graff; Emmanuel and Sophie Guillaume; Joel Arthur Rosenthal and Pierre Jeannet of JAR; Stanley B. Kahn of Kahn Jewelers; Amir Khazaneh; Neil Lane; Fred Leighton, Pat Saling, and Rebecca Selva of Fred Leighton; Elsa Peretti; Paloma Picasso; Janis Savitt of M + J Savitt; Rachelle Epstein of Shelle; Peter, Paul, and Mark Schaffer of A La Vieille Russie; Anthony Hopenhajm and Roshi Ameri of Seaman Schepps; Peter Schneirla; Saralee Smithwick of Smithwick Dillon; Donna M. Sturm; Pierce B. MacGuire and Nicolas Bongard of Schlumberger at Tiffany; Frank Arcaro, Annamarie Sandecki, archivist, and Fernanda K. Gilligan, senior vice president, public relations, of Tiffany; John Ullmann; Veronique Ma'Arop of Van Cleef & Arpels; Paul Vartanian and Heidi Fritzsche of Vartanian & Sons; Edward Landrigan, Maria Kelleher-Williams, and Brigid Leary of Verdura; Geoffrey Munn and Katherine Purcell of Wartski; Stanley Silberstein of David Webb; Christopher Walling and Dorota Porebska-Brozyna of Christopher Walling; Laurence S. Krashes of Harry Winston; and Robert M. Gibson of Raymond C. Yard. The modern leather boxes on the cover were kindly provided by Leslie Tcheyan of Tryon Mercantile, Inc. We would like to make special mention of two jewelers, Julius Cohen and Alfred Montezinos, who passed away during the writing of this book; their memory and effervescence continues in our hearts and work.

The auction houses are archaeological trenches for jewelry historians. Both Christie's and Sotheby's were unfailingly gracious in fielding our requests. We achieved greater breadth in our research through the ministrations of François Curiel, Simon Teakle, Susan Berg, Myriam Debaty, Kathy Kermian, Dianne Lewis, Eric Valdieu, and Anne Choate at Christie's, and at Sotheby's, John D. Block, David Bennett, Valerie Vlasaty, Eve J. Reppen, Jacqueline Fay, Arianna Pagani, Jessica Deutsch, Lynn Pearson, and Richard Buckley.

The following jewelry historians and gemologists gave us invaluable assistance from the reservoirs of their specialized knowledge: Sigrid Barten; C. P. "Cap" Beesley of the American Gemological Laboratories; Shirley Bury; Françoise Cailles; Mary Murphy, Michael Koch; Frederik Schwarz; Viviane Jutheau; Bernard Morel; Elise B. Misiorowski, research librarian of the GIA; Diana Scarisbrick; Jonathan Snellenburg; Janet Zapata; and Benjamin Zucker.

Our text and picture research was facilitated by an impassioned and steadfast group of archivists, curators, librarians, photographers, and picture editors: Janet Lorenz of the Margaret Herrick Library at the Academy of Motion Picture Arts and Sciences; Arnold Newman; Katherine G. Bang and Peter Rohowsky of the Bettmann Archives; Dr. Roderick Bladel of the Billy Rose Theatre Collection at the New York Library for the Performing Arts at Lincoln Center; Felicity Murdo-Smith, press secretary to the Queen, at Buckingham Palace Press Office; Diana Edkins and Don Osterweil at Condé Nast; Margaret Kelly, director, and Robyn Tromer, assistant curator, of the Forbes Magazine Collection; Betty Galella of Ron Galella Photography; Mary Hilliard; Jean Howard; Allan Goodrich, audiovisual archivist, of the John F. Kennedy Library; Andy Marcus of Fred Marcus Photography; Robert Tuggle, director, Gail Frohlinger, costume curator, and John Pennino, assistant archivist, of the Metropolitan Opera Archives; Sonja Edare, Chantal Bizot, and Evelyne Possémé of the Musée des

Arts Décoratifs; Mary Corliss and Terry Geesken of the Museum of Modern Art Film Stills Archive; Beth Draper and Howard Davis of the N. W. Ayer Archives; Ann Tortorelli, syndication representative, and Maureen Fulton, manager, of *People* Magazine Syndication and Letters; Alberto Rizzo; Robert Sherbow; Catherine Cheval of Roger-Viollet; Gerard Stora of the Wildenstein Gallery; James Smeal; Russell C. Feather, museum specialist, Department of Mineral Sciences, National Museum of Natural History, Smithsonian Institution; Eric Weiss; Jorge Jaramillo of Wide World Photos; Karen Robinovitz, Syndication, of *Women's Wear Daily*. When rare-book dealer Shaun Gunson died during the course of our research, we lost our direct link for hard-to-find jewelry publications. His work on our behalf is irreplaceable.

We would like to give special thanks to the Diamond Information Center, which has been so supportive of this project. Partner Alyse Frankenberg was diligent and thoughtful in her role as liaison. Senior Partner Joan Parker was courteous and encouraging throughout the long process.

Lynn Ramsey, president/CEO of the Jewelry Information Center (JIC), was instrumental in getting this project under way. Without her passion for diamonds and jewelry, as well as her confidence in the idea, it may never have seen the light of day. Connor Strauss, David Fardon, and Heather S. Quayle of Argyle Diamonds generously provided us with material on the Australian pink diamonds. Public relations gurus Carol Bohdan, Janie Elder, Linda Goldstein of Linda Goldstein Public Relations, Ian D. MacKintosh at Eleanor Lambert Ltd., Chen Sam, and Robert Wolf smoothed our path with information, photographs, and, when necessary, troubleshooting.

The contributions of the Esmerian and the King families, Alix Alexander, Diana Anderson, Rosemary Ewing, Stephanie Guest and Richard Ellis, Shelley Wanger, Joan Quinn, Tommie Ridder, and Lyn Revson have immeasurably improved the book. Mrs. H. Bradley Martin, Lucy Broido, Carol Butz, Rayed Fouad Gahli, Sean Ferrer, Richard J. Hutto, Beth Kulick, Marion Lambert, Louise Parrish, François du Sardou, and Susan Springer deserve special mention for their unique additions. Literary agent Nancy Trichter masterfully guided the book through the preliminary stages.

We are grateful to Mark Mayfield, our favorite editor-in-chief of *Art & Antiques*, and the discriminating editor-in-chief Gary Walther and the indomitable managing editor Kathleen Fitzpatrick of *Departures* for giving us the opportunity to develop some of our ideas in print for their beautiful magazines. We worked out other ideas in lectures and workshops. For supporting the spoken word and works in progress, we thank Helene Fortunoff and all the presidents and members of the Women's Jewelry Association (WJA), Linde Meyer, the Saint Louis Art Museum, and the Museum of Art and Archaeology at the University of Missouri-Columbia.

The kindness of Trudy Tripolone on a day-to-day basis gave us freedom to develop our themes. Our family and friends did stand by us in the years it took to complete this project. We would like to mention Carolyn Cornish, Landt and Lisl Dennis, Trudie Fasel and Kimberley Fasel, Hilda Janssens, Robert McDonald Parker, Audrey Proddow, Stan Schnier, John Stevens, Michael Aram Wolohojian, and Suneet Varma. A heartfelt expression of gratitude goes to George Fasel, who helped us get off the rope bridge with the piano intact and then showed us how to make it sing.

David Behl, the photographer responsible for the original images of jewelry throughout the book, gave generously of his time. His photographs show a peerless technical skill and artistry in capturing the beauty of diamonds.

At Abrams, the queries and comments of editor Lory Frankel, who has become the expert editor for jewelry historians, inspired us all over again. Not one but two picture editors, Neil Ryder Hoos and Catherine Ruello, handled our varied images. The first round was managed by Hoos, who kept us up-to-date and organized. Ruello "threaded the needle," and her insight into the visual run made the Jewelers' Gallery a reality. Designer Carol Robson transformed her knowledge, sensitivity, and outright love of jewelry into an original layout. Director of Special Projects Bob Morton was at once patient, humorous, and understanding of the unique complexities that assembling and writing a history of precious jewelry entails. With Morton at the helm, it was smooth sailing all the way.

PENNY PRODDOW
MARION FASEL
NEW YORK CITY, 1996

PHOTOGRAPH CREDITS

The publisher and authors wish to thank the jewelers, auctions houses, private collectors, and museums named in the captions for supplying the necessary photographs. Other photograph credits are listed below by page number.

David Behl: 2–3 (Jewelry Courtesy Fred Leighton), 20, 26, 28–30, 32, 34, 37 center, 39, 40, 42–44, 46–47, 56, 58 left, 62, 64, 68–69 bottom, 72 center and bottom, 74, 80, 81 center, 83, 90, 92, 124, 126, 128 (Jewelry Courtesy Fred Leighton), 130, 134, 138 top, 139, 141 left, 143, 149–151, 153–155, 160 bottom, 161, 163, 167, 168 (Jewerly Courtesy Fred Leighton), 171; © David Behl: 10, 60, 67 left, 78, 86, 87 top, 105, 112, 115 right, 118, 131, 144; Berthaud: 16, 22, 79 bottom; Bettmann Archive/Bettmann Newsphotos, New York: 55, 67 right, 72 top, 73, 79 top, 84 left, 115 left, 119, 133; Bibliothèque Nationale de France, Paris: 15, 18; Courtesy François Cailles, *René Boivin, Jeweler*, Quartet Books, Ltd, 1994: 85, 176 bottom; Courtesy Boucheron: 173 top; Courtesy Bulgari: 136 (photograph by Gaio Bacci), 180 center; Courtesy Cartier Archives: 174 bottom, 175 top and center; Cartier Collection, Geneva: 180 top; Christie's Geneva: 52, 122; Christie's, London: 19; Christie's, New York: 53, 84 right, 170 top; Christie's St. Moritz: 170 bottom; Courtesy Julius Cohen, Jeweler: 114, 123, 179 left; Collingwood's: 17; Courtesy Paul Flato: 176 top; Henri Vever Papers, Freer Gallery of Art and Arthur M. Sackler Gallery Archives, Smithsonian Institution, Washington, D. C.: 174 right; Horst: 87 bottom (Courtesy *Vogue*), 91 (Courtesy *Vogue* Copyright © renewed 1969) by The Condé Nast Publications Inc.); Courtesy *Harper's Bazaar* © 1958: 125; Courtesy Jean Howard, *Travels with Cole Porter*, Harry N. Abrams, Inc., 1991: 176 left; Hulton Deutsch Collection Limited, London: 48; Courtesy *Interview*: 137; André Kertesz, © Kertesz Estate (Courtesy *Vogue*): 76; Eliot Elisofon/*Life Magazine*, © Time Inc.: 178 center; Fred Marcus Photography/Andy Marcus (Courtesy Harry Winston) : 158 bottom; Courtesy Mrs. H. Bradley Martin: 23; The Board of Trustees of the National Museums and Galleries of Merseyside, Lady Lever Art Gallery, Port Sunlight, England: 41; Arnold Newman: 181 top; © 1977 *Newsweek*, Inc. All Rights Reserved, Reprinted by permission, photograph by Alberto Rizzo: 141 right; General Research Division, The New York Public Library: 49; John Burns/The New York Times Pictures: 138 bottom; Irving Penn: 120 (Courtesy *Vogue*, copyright 1956 by The Condé Nast Publications Inc.), 166 (Courtesy *Vogue*, copyright 1994 by The Condé Nast Publications Inc.); *People Weekly* © 1993 Robert Sherbow: 164 right; Courtesy Private Collection: 6 (photograph by Zindman/Fremont, New York) 33, 93 (photograph by Zindman/Fremont, New York); R.M.N., Paris, © Musée National du Château, Compiègne: 12; Retna Ltd, NYC: 96, 98; © Roger-Viollet, Paris: 21, 61, 108; Courtesy of Seaman Schepps: 179 bottom; Frederik Schwarz: 14; Sheeler: 65 (Courtesy *Vogue* © 1927); Craig Skinner/Celebrity Photo © 1993 All Rights Reserved: 158 top right; James Smeal/Ron Galella Ltd: 157, 159 top right (© 1992) and top left, 162 (© 1995); Sotheby's, Geneva: 50–51, 132 bottom; Sotheby's, New York: 110, 156 (© 1994); © Edward Steichen Estate: 66 (Courtesy *Vanity Fair*/General Research Division, The New York Public Library), 70 (Courtesy *Vogue*); By permission of Tiffany & Co. All Rights Reserved: 24, 116, 121, 160 top (photograph by Louis Irizarry), 173 bottom, 178 bottom, 180 bottom, 182 top (photograph by Walter Chin); Courtesy Van Cleef & Arpels: 88 (photograph by Laurent Sully Jaulmes), 107, 109, 178 top; *Vanity Fair* © 1931 (renewed 1942, 1946, 1949, 1959) by The Condé Nast Publications, Inc.: 69 top; Courtesy Verdura, New York: 177 top, 177 bottom (photograph by Horst); Copyright © 1953 Twentieth Century Fox Film Corporation. All Rights Reserved: 94; Courtesy Christopher Walling: 152; Courtesy Harry Winston: 101, 102, 106; *Women's Wear Daily*: 140, 158 left, 159 bottom, 168 bottom, 182 bottom; Courtesy Raymond C. Yard: 175 bottom